D0901327

FALLING
FOR
MONEY

How to Have a Lifetime
Love Affair with your
Finances

Krisstina Wise

Published by Krisstina Wise

ISBN: 978-0692560907

Copyright © 2015 Krisstina Wise. All rights reserved. Printed in the United States of America. No part of this publication may be reproduced or distributed in any form or by any means, or stored in a database or retrieval system, except as permitted under Sections 107 or 108 of the U.S. Copyright Act, without prior written permis sion of the publisher. This book is printed on acid free paper.

Material in this book is for educational purposes only. This product is sold with the understanding that neither any of the authors nor the publisher are engaged in rendering legal, accounting, investment, or any other pro fessional service specifically suited to one particular individual's needs who may be reading this book. Neither the publisher nor the authors assume any liability for any errors or omissions or for how this book or its contents are used or interpreted or for any consequences resulting directly or indirectly from the use of this book.

The views expressed by the individuals in this book do not necessarily reflect the views shared by the companies they are employed by (or the companies mentioned in this book). The employment status and affiliations of the authors with the companies referenced are subject to change.

CONTENTS

This book is dedicated to my amazing family:

To my husband, Garry. You have lived your vows to stick together through sickness and health. I wouldn't have made it through 2013 without you, my love. Thank you for being my partner in a co-invented good life.

To my beautiful children, Kael and Macy. You make me a proud mom. I love you. It's now your turn to spread your wings and design and live your own good life stories.

To my parents, Dad, Judy and Mom. Thank you for your love of me and for the support of my crazy good life dreams and endeavors.

To my goodLife Companies family. You each inspire me every day. It's an honor to work with you as we dream, invent and build a good life for ourselves, our families and our customers.

Sex and Money: two things our culture is obsessed with having, but not improving. There's not much I can do for your sex life, but I'm nearly certain I can improve your money life.

I am Krisstina Wise and I have a deeply-held passion and commitment for designing and living a good life. I'm the lucky wife of the best husband in the world, and the proud mom of the finest children on the planet. I am also Founder and CEO of a multimillion-dollar enterprise, the goodLife Companies.

Comprised of four successful brands, the goodLife Companies consist of GoodLife Realty, GoodLife Mortgage, The Paperless Agent, and Wealthy*Wellthy*. The first three serve the real estate industry, while the fourth—my newest brand—was created to help women learn to love money so that they can live a happy, financially free, good life.

Nationally recognized as leaders in their fields, my brands have been featured by major companies such as Apple, Evernote, and USA Today. But despite their success and notoriety, all my brands blossomed from just a dream; I started with the same basics that you will learn about in this book.

Falling for Money is, as you'd guess, about money (and, perhaps, just a little bit about sex). In writing this book, my goal was to teach others how they can have a lifetime love affair with money so that they can feel good about making it, talking about it and creating wealth with it. Within these pages, I've provided a proven methodology for dreaming about money, planning for it, spending it, and ultimately getting rich with it in order to live a goodLife. If you are not already, I say it's your turn to be head over heels in love, in a healthy relationship with your finances.

As you know, there is no shortage of books, articles and programs on the subject of money. But you probably also know this: if you've read one of those books, you've pretty much read them all. I've delved into numerous best-selling money books, and not a single one provided the knowledge readers really need to take full control of their personal fiscal affairs.

In Falling for Money I approach the subject of money from a different angle. This book contains my real-life philosophy and practices for earning, saving, and investing enough money to live a goodLife—a balanced life filled with laughter and happiness, passion and ambition, and, most importantly, a life free from financial stress. Falling for Money starts by asking yourself the philosophical question, "How much money is enough?" Only by knowing how much is enough to live the life we want can we go about developing a healthy, long-lasting relationship with money that brings joy and happiness that we want instead of the stress and anxiety, and at times shame, we often feel.

As you read, please keep in mind that I have written this book as a confab. I don't claim to be a financial guru, financial planner, or any kind of financial authority. The pages that follow result from being repeatedly asked over the years for "money advice." I'm sharing with you here the same informal, private conversations that I've had with hundreds of others—most of whom later suggested that I write a book, because the advice I offered had changed their lives for the better.

Even though a plethora of information exists about financial principles, I think we as a nation need all the education we can get on the subject. In America we're not taught personal money principles, skills, and practices in school—not even when spending tens of thousands of dollars to earn an MBA or Ph.D.

As a result, we acquire financial habits from common cultural practices, often following destructive customs that eventually lead us to a place of financial instability.

Ultimately, I believe that most Americans don't know what it really takes to create a goodLife; instead, we try to live a lifestyle that we cannot afford. In fact, I venture to say that about 95% of us can be lumped into that category, whether we know it or not.

You will soon understand why I make this bold claim. But for now, just go with the following logic: if you are reading this book, then you are interested in financial self-improvement. If you are interested in financial self-improvement, then you are in one of three groups:

You know that you belong to the 95% attempting to live an unaffordable lifestyle, and are here to gather the knowledge, skills and practices for changing that;

You are among the other 5%, and are here to improve skills that can help amplify your financial success or increase your velocity towards financial independence; or

You currently deem yourself in the 5%, but learn through the exercises offered that what you thought isn't necessarily the case.

My hope is that, no matter which group you fit into, you'll acquire life-changing knowledge in this philosophical and practical guide. My methodology for designing, creating, and affording a goodLife has five steps. Each step is divided into several parts and exercises, making the material simple to follow and easy to understand. Most important, it allows you to move forward with incremental and actionable steps allowing for growth and change for a brighter financial future.

The steps are:

Step 1: Reflecting on My goodLife
Step 2: Setting My goodLife Goals
Step 3: Money Mapping My goodLife
Step 4: Generating My goodLife Income
Step 5: Establishing goodPractices for a goodLife

Congratulations on being among the brave few to find yourself at such a momentous starting point. One of my favorite proverbs is: "The best time to plant a tree is twenty years ago. The second best time is now."

As I continue my journey to actualizing my own goodLife and good-Business, I invite you to join me. There's a lot to be accomplished to set you on your own path to designing, planning, and living a goodLife, so let's get to it.

p.s. You may (or may not) recognize that I've left out an important part of my story. This was an intentional omission. I recognized, as I sat down to write that chapter, that it demanded to be its own book if I wanted to do it justice. That's just what I've decided to do, so book two is coming soon.

Chapter I

Step 1: Reflecting on My goodLife

"Without reflection, we blindly go on our way, creating more unintended consequences, and failing to achieve anything useful."

Margaret J. Wheatley

Be honest: when did you last take time by yourself and for yourself? Step 1 of the goodLife Money Mapping System™ urges you to sit back, relax, and reflect. Reflection allows you to take an important glimpse into your own life. You might even try closing your eyes as you visualize what in your life is good, bad, and really bad.

Find a quiet space—alone—where you can begin your reflection by asking a simple philosophical question: "What is a goodLife to me?" Reflect on all the areas of your life—what I call the six F-words: Family, Finances, Fitness, Fun, Flourish, and Faith. Continue on by assessing which areas of your life satisfy you, and which could use some improvement in the coming year.

As part of the exercise in this chapter, you'll be answering questions such as these: *Am I satisfied? Am I dissatisfied? How am I doing in each life category individually? How am I doing in each individual category as it collectively relates to life concerns?*

As we begin, I want you to know that there is only one rule: Be nice to yourself. Often we are too quick to judge ourselves negatively, so I am simply disallowing it.

You are perfect just the way you are right now. If you discover that you wish to grow into a different perfect person, then that's part of the work we will do together.

Not too long ago, when I was going through a significant (and very difficult) time of change, I was one of my harshest critics. Anna, a dear friend, offered me an eloquent metaphor. "Krisstina," she said, "you are like the caterpillar about to change into a butterfly. You're perfect as a caterpillar—and you'll be perfect as a butterfly. But when you become the butterfly, you'll have wings and be able to fly."

Any time you catch yourself in negative self-talk, just stop, take a deep breath, and say these words: "I am perfect just the way I am." If you intend on keeping this promise, I want you to write the following words:

I promise NOT to judge myself while reading this book.

Everything I am sharing with you moving forward is based on lessons learned and beliefs and practices that I hold at this point in my life. Everything I ask of you in this book, I also ask of myself.

I am just like you. I am a human being doing my best at being human. I have produced some great successes. But I've made far more mistakes. I have experienced pure joy to a place where I thought my heart might burst, but I have also had my heart broken to a point that I felt I could never recover. I now have a successful marriage to a husband who loves, adores, and cherishes me (and I him). However, I once had an abusive marriage that sucked every bit of self-love and self-worth out of every cell of my body.

I am a good mother, reflected in the admirable character of my two teenage children and the close relationship I have with them both. But there was a time when I was an awful mother, spending more time caring about my success than about their well-being. I've been a picture-perfect example of health, but I've also been so wretchedly sick that I came severely close to death.

But that's life, isn't it? The lifelong journey is a contrast of ups and downs. Although we wish to avoid the downs, it is through struggle that the gate to self-actualization opens. It is in reflecting upon our hurt, pain, suffering, mistakes, and failures that we discover what opposites we desire.

Goal-setting and dream boards are common practices these days as exercises to start off a new year. These are great and absolutely necessary practices. In fact, you will complete both of these exercises in the next chapter as Step 2 of the goodLife Money Mapping System™. However, my own life experience has led to me to believe that there is an imperative step to take before setting future goals and making future plans. The step before goal-setting and dreaming is reflecting. As a starting point, we must examine what we do that works for us in aspiring to live a goodLife. We must equally acknowledge that what is not working, if continued, will thwart our best intentions for living a balanced, happy, healthy, productive life.

In reflecting on my own life, I look at six life categories. Calling them my six F-words helps me easily remember them:

Faith

The word faith can be interchanged here for the word spirituality. I use the word faith, because, independent of one's religious beliefs or spiritual practices, there comes a point after much assessing, planning, and preparing where we have to let go and just have faith that things will work out the way they are meant to. It took me a long time to realize this; once I did, I let go of trying to control so much of life that simply isn't controllable. As a former self-proclaimed "perfectionist," it was with this release that I finally found happiness.

Family | Friends

We tend to think of family as relatives—those people we are affiliated with by blood. I, however, broaden that definition. Because I was loved by a man who chose to be my father, who married my mother even though she was pregnant with another man's child, I consider family as those who choose to love us for who we are. Thinking of family in this way certainly includes more people, but it can also eliminate negative influences if need be. Just because we share the same gene pool with some people doesn't mean they have to be in our life.

Finances

This F-word is about money: earning, spending, saving, and investing it. Being financially healthy means living a life we can afford, which not only assumes that you have income and no personal debt, but also suf-ficient savings and investments. I've lost a lot of money in my life because I was ignorant of the principles money requires if it's to be kept and grown. For years I was an "Income-Rich Poor Person," which means I was concerned mostly with the number of zeros (following any number on my income statement. Now, knowing better, I focus more on the number of zeros on my balance sheet.

We're also going to talk about how money is earned. Many people don't think of income this way, but we earn equal to the amount of perceived value we offer to an employer or a customer. This value is expressed, respectively, as a wage or as the price of a product/service. In business, the number of potential customers who are aware of our valuable product/service also affects our perceived value. At the end of the day, if we do not live the lifestyle we want, it's because we do not produce enough value.

Fitness | Food

Fitness means exercise and food means diet, but this life category also includes everything considered to be "self-care." In other words, regular exercise, proper diet and nutrition, appropriate rest and recovery, and regular preventative medical examinations, as well as other self-care appointments, such as acupuncture, massage and therapy. Yes, I said the word therapy. I used to think only those who had emotional or relational problems visited therapists. Today I consider therapy to be a valuable part of self-care and personal/relational growth.

Meditation is another important self-care area. Meditation could also fit in the "Faith" category if it's used to connect spiritually—I do use meditation for that reason also—but here I mean mindful meditation for the sake of a daily check-in with the mind and body. It's important to take a "time-out" from the daily grind to simply *be*. Finally, one of the biggest areas of self-care is the conscious awareness and management of stress. Stress is a killer, literally. It nearly killed me, literally.

Fun

Fun means taking a break from life's responsibilities. It could mean enjoying hobbies like golfing, painting or gardening. It could be as mindless as immersing oneself into a non-fiction book, stretching out in a hammock and gazing at the stars, or hanging out with friends at a tailgate party. Before I got sick, I considered going to the office to be weekend fun. I took vacations, but not anywhere that wasn't wireless. I love what I do, but to be at it twenty-four seven isn't healthy. I learned that the hard way; not taking time off contributed significantly to my physical and mental crash. Today, my husband and I take plenty of time for fun. We find it snuggled up to a book (or each other at our new lake house)—acquired for the simple reason of putting bona fide fun and relaxation into our life. Fun (and sex! is one of the best stress relievers.

Flourish

I live by a credo: "I am either becoming, or just becoming old." To always be becoming means I must always be learning and growing. A goodLife requires it. Otherwise, we are insured eventual stagnation and, at best, mediocrity. To flourish means to thrive. To thrive means to reach our God-given potential—never settling for anything less than becoming our best possible self—which is simple, but not necessarily easy. It takes commitment, discipline, action, and grace.

Exercise 1: My goodLife Reflection

The goal of this exercise is to gain an honest perspective of your current situation.

Instructions:

1. Find a quiet spot, alone and away from distraction. Turn off your phone, email, Facebook and anything else that might interrupt this quiet time.

2. For each of the six F-words (below), write down your answer to "What is a good life to me?"

3. Are you are satisfied or dissatisfied with your current situation in each category? Dissatisfied here means that you are unhappy enough that you are willing to make a change this year.
    - What are your biggest successes?
    - What are your recurrent failures?
    - Do you have good habits and practices, poor ones, or none at all?
    - Why do you think you continue to fall flat in some areas of your life?

4. Rate your F-words on a scale from A-F:
    - Give yourself an F if you feel you are failing. Absolute change is necessary.
    - Give yourself a C if you feel that you're not awful—but not great, either. You may wish to make changes.
    - Give yourself an A if you feel you are succeeding and/or excelling. No change necessary.

5. In areas where you are dissatisfied, write down what changes you need to make this year to bring you one step closer to living your ultimate goodLife.

ex. 01

Faith

What is a goodLife to me when it comes to my faith? Where do I feel fulfilled in my faith? Where am I lacking? Do I have good habits and practices to keep me centered in my faith? What habits could I change or create to feel better about my connection to my higher power? What do I try to control in my life that I can let go of this year, offering it up to faith? What goals did I set in this area last year that I achieved? What goals did I not achieve? How do I feel about this? What will I change this year to feel more balanced and fulfilled in my faith?

I give myself a(n) [A]   [B]   [C]   [D]   [F]   (circle one)
in the area of my faith and spirituality.

Family | Friends

What is a goodLife to me when it comes to my family? Do I feel loved for who I am (and who I am not)? How do I rate my relationship with my spouse/partner? What could I do to improve it? Do I love, honor, and respect my spouse/partner? Does my partner love, honor, and respect me? How is my relationship with my children? Could it be better? If so, how? How's my relationship with my parents, siblings, and other close relatives? Do I have deep meaningful friendships? Do I offer enough time to my family and friends so that I feel fulfilled? What goals did I set in this area last year that I achieved? What goals did I not achieve? How do I feel about this? What will I change this year to feel more balanced and fulfilled with my family's concerns?

I give myself a(n) [A]   [B]   [C]   [D]   [F]   (circle one)
in the area of my family and friends.

Finances

What is a goodLife to me when it comes to money? How do I define my relationship with money? Love/hate? Passive/aggressive? Passionate/Respectful?   Healthy/unhealthy? How much money is

ex. 01

enough? Am I satisfied with the amount of my/family annual income? What are my beliefs about money? Do my current beliefs hurt or help me? Does my spouse/partner share my money beliefs/habits? Do we have a lot of conflict over money? If so, why? How much money do I have saved? How much money does my family have saved? How much do I/we have invested? Is it enough? How much more income do I wish to earn this year? How will I earn it? Am I happy with the state of my career or business? Does my current career or business produce enough money to live the life I want? What are my biggest career/business successes? Do I have any recurrent failures? What goals did I set in this area last year that I achieved? What goals did I not achieve? How do I feel about this? What will I change this year to feel more in control of my money, my career, and my business?

I give myself a(n) [A] [B] [C] [D] [F] (circle one)
in the area of money, finances, and career.

Fitness | Food
Do I have a consistent exercise practice? If yes, is it sufficient to meet my fitness goals? If no, why not? Do I have a healthy diet? What do I consistently eat that is unhealthy and sabotages my health and weight goals? Do I get an annual physical, mammogram, and/or other preventative exams and tests? Am I stressed too often? What goals did I set in this area last year that I achieved? What goals did I not achieve? How do I feel about this? What will I change this year to take better care of myself? What will I change to feel more fit and healthy?

I give myself a(n) [A] [B] [C] [D] [F] (circle one)
in the area of fitness and self-care.

ex. 01

Fun

Do I regularly take time off to have fun? Do I rest and recover? How often do I take a planned vacation? When was the last time I took a "real" vacation that was truly enjoyable and not stressful? What do I like to do for fun? What are my hobbies? Do I spend enough time enjoying them? Do I spend quality time with myself? Do I spend too much time having fun so that it gets in the way of achieving my goals? What goals did I set in this area last year that I achieved? What goals did I not achieve? How do I feel about this? What will I change this year to feel more fun, relaxed and happy?

I give myself a(n) [A] [B] [C] [D] [F] (circle one)
in the area of fun, relaxation, and time off.

Flourish

Is my life flourishing? Is my career/business flourishing? If not, why not? What would have to happen for me to feel accomplished, fulfilled, and successful in all areas of my life? Am I becoming, or just becoming old? How much do I spend on personal development? Do I invest enough time and money in personal knowledge, education or training? How many books do I read per year? What books should I read next? Do I feel that I would do better in other areas of my life if I learned better practices for success? What areas of my life do I feel stagnant in and therefore wish to expand? What books can I read? In what areas of life could I use help to make that part of my life more fulfilling? What goals did I set in this area last year that I achieved? What goals did I not achieve? How do I feel about this? What will I change about me this year that will require help from people or books?

I give myself a(n) [A] [B] [C] [D] [F] (circle one)
in the area of my flourishing personal development

ex. 01

Recap:

How did that feel? This is a philosophical exercise, so there is no right or wrong answer. It's likely that, by doing this exercise, you'll find that you are out of balance. For example, you may be excelling in one category, but mark yourself as failing in another. Or you may feel as though you dedicate an inordinate amount of time to one category while ignoring another. Don't worry. This is normal. In fact, it's great news! Only by contemplating our current situation and reflecting on what led us to where we are right now can we learn what we need to know to move into a new situation—the future.

I cannot emphasize enough the importance of the reflection stage of annual planning and goal-setting. It's not just grunt work: I still do it each year as a way to "check-in." I congratulate myself on my successes, I contemplate the reasons behind my failures, and then I incorporate my realizations into creating the most powerful and meaningful plan possible for the next year. Don't you want your efforts to be just as effective?

THOUGHTS & NOTES

ex. 01

THOUGHTS & NOTES

_____
_____
_____
_____
_____
_____
_____
_____
_____
_____
_____
_____
_____
_____
_____
_____
_____
_____
_____
_____
_____
_____
_____
_____

ex. 01

Chapter II

Step 2: Setting My goodLife Goals

"I can teach anybody how to get what
they want out of life. The problem is that
I can't find anybody who can tell me what
they want."

Mark Twain

Before I jump into Step 2, let me ask: how did you do with the "Be Kind to Yourself" rule in Step 1? Were you kind—or did you judge yourself? Even if you didn't completely eliminate that negative self-talk, congratulations on becoming aware of it! In the future, continue replacing that kind of negativity with these words: "I am perfect exactly as I am."

Now that you've reflected on your life to date (without judgment), you can turn to inventing your dreamLife. From this vision you will establish your goodLife goals and work to actualize them in the coming year.

Step Two includes two parts:
Visualizing your dreamLife
Setting your goodLife goals

Visualizing my dreamLife

"Visualizing your dreamLife" requires more reflection, but instead of thinking about the life you currently have, you'll visualize the life you want. As part of the work in "Setting your goodLife Goals," you'll distill your dreamLife vision into actionable goals for the year ahead. Achieving those goals will bring you one step closer to living your dreamLife.

Most people I know sit in one of two camps, both of which can equally stifle any real opportunity to live the lifestyle they want:

They quit dreaming
or
They dream but never act

As kids, we were all good at make-believe. But somewhere in adulthood, in the day-to-day practicality of living, most of us lose our ability to dream.

I feel sad for those who stop dreaming. I've noticed that people who lose sight of their dreams become cynical, pessimistic and disenchanted. I believe that staying connected to the ability to dream is a prerequisite to creating a goodLife filled with health and happiness. Our dream inspires and fuels our passion for life, giving us purpose, direction and focus. It's the dream that drives us to persevere through both easy and the difficult times.

On the other hand, some people create exquisite dream boards, are disciples of the Law of Attraction and maintain a positive attitude—yet never see their dreams realized. It's certainly not from any lack of dreaming or trying on their part, but dreams cannot become reality unless we take the appropriate actions to cause and enact our desired future. In other words, dreaming and wishing aren't enough. Action is required. We can begin actualizing our dreams through a practice of personal goal-setting followed by goal achieving.

Few know this, but I came home from the hospital to a single-wide trailer home, where I spent the first several years of my life. I grew up in a small, under-educated town and lived my youth in the part of society labeled as the working-class poor [see figure 1]. Both my father and mother were alcoholics, choosing the bottle over my brother and me. Their lifestyle led to divorce and, sadly, the eventual abandonment of their adolescent children.

Because I was on my own as a naive young girl, I encountered more than my fair share of trauma. As an adult, I've had therapists ask me how I was able to survive so many horrific childhood events. I could never come up with a compelling answer, but I now believe that my ability to dream enabled me to endure. I dreamed of a better life, a life that was good—my goodLife.

My need to survive as a child solidified my talent for visualizing and dreaming. I've sometimes heard people whisper, "She never could have dreamed that she would be where she is today, consider-

[figure 1]

ing where she came from." What they didn't know is that I did dream it. I dreamed of my goodLife, and then set out to actualize it.

As you visualize your dreams and set your goals, keep in mind that your dreamLife is the life you wish to be living sometime in the distant future. It is the end you work backwards from to create goals for the more immediate future—specifically for this book, and for the next twelve months.

In the following exercise, I encourage you to design big, but remember that your dreamLife is not meant to be a fantasy forever. The magic here lies in the balancing act between our ability to hold a dream and to plan achievable goals for realizing that dream. We might not always want to live in the present, but it's important that we don't wait to enjoy our life until some unknown time in the future.

Living your present life in the future is what I call "future-tripping." I used to spend most of my life future-tripping—the major reason I wasn't the mother I could have been. I might have been present physically, but I wasn't there mentally or emotionally. The life-saving ability that enabled me to survive as a child was destructive as an adult. To escape the pain of the present in my childhood, I learned to live in the future. Consequently, I sacrificed some of life's most precious moments as an adult, especially with my young children, because I was so busy planning, working and living for the future.

Future-tripping is just as destructive to your future as not having a dream at all. I consciously remind myself that I want to be present each moment of each day and experience life as a journey in pursuit of attaining the dream. To avoid the temptation to disregard my current life in favor of future-tripping, I use this goodLife credo: "Wherever I am, be there."

Here are some examples in the six F-word categories to help you envision your own dreamLife:

Faith

I have faith in my life's purpose and believe in a universe far bigger than I. I meditate and connect with my higher power every day. I feel love. I express love. I practice forgiveness—of myself and others—and am free of anger, resentment, and hostility. I attend a spiritual service once per week.

Family | Friends

I love, honor, and cherish my husband for who he is and who he isn't. I tell my husband and kids that I love them each day. I am cherished by my children and grandchildren, and I spend good quality time with them, as well as enjoy time with close friends and family with whom I have deep, meaningful relationships.

Finances

The business enterprise generates $7,500,000 in revenue and profits annually. At retirement, our personal net worth is valued at $25,000,000 and generates $1,500,000 of income after taxes per year. All of our financial instruments are in place: wills, trusts, insurance policies, and investment/retirement accounts. We are 100% debt free and our in-come affords us a lifestyle of global five-star travel, a modern home on the lake in Austin, Texas, and a quaint oceanfront home in the Caribbean. We have access to the best health care available and to leading self-care practitioners. We enjoy having the ability to donate generously to philanthropic causes we believe in.

Fitness | Food

I am optimally healthy—mentally, emotionally, and physically—which enables me to engage in my life fully. I not only *feel* healthy and happy, but *look* healthy and happy as well. I am at my desired weight of ___ and enjoy a consistent exercise practice that includes yoga, running, and moderate weight-training. I follow a Paleo-diet philosophy practice. I look great for my age and feel years younger than I am.

Fun

I enjoy regular quiet weekend trips to the lake house, including peaceful time on my paddleboard and time with family and friends semi-annually at the Caribbean house. I enjoy annual global travel with my husband, and girl's trips with close friends. I regularly make time for my hobbies of golf and painting.

Flourish

I live in a mood of uncertainty which is the source that powers my perpetual love of learning. I read at least two non-fiction books per month. I have fun conversing in my second language during trips to Spanish-speaking countries. I attend a minimum of one learning-based conference each year, enjoying the never-ending opportunity to meet new people with different beliefs, ideas, and customs. These events enhance my perspective on life. I feel fulfilled and that I am flourishing in all areas of my life. I am happy.

Exercise 2.1: Visualizing My dreamLife

This exercise is your chance to let your imagination go wild. Start by giving yourself permission to daydream. I want you to find a comfortable spot, close your eyes and visualize a future you want. Make it an action-oriented film that you play in your head. Use all of your senses and experience it as if every bit of it were real.

This may seem foolish, but I encourage you to do it nonetheless. Studies in neuroscience have proven that our primal brain does not know the difference between what's imagined and what's real. Proof of this is experienced in a movie theatre. Have you ever gotten choked up or cried during a movie? You know what's happening in the movie isn't real, yet your nervous system reacts otherwise. By engaging in this dream-building exercise, you will generate new synapses in your brain that literally build a new space of possibility in your mind.

To help you get started, imagine what your goodLife looks like as if it were happening right now. Who's in it? Where do you live? What do you drive? What do you see? Is it warm or cold outside? Can you feel the air on your skin? What do you smell? What are you eating? What do you taste? What do you look like? What emotions are you feeling? Can you feel the magic of the universe around you? Are you smiling? Are you laughing?

Instructions:

1. Take five minutes or fifty. It's up to you. My only request that you complete this exercise.

2. When you finish, take your vision and transfer your dreams into each of the six F-word life categories in the space below. Refer to the previous examples for help.

ex. 02.1

Faith _____

_____

_____

_____

Family & Friends _____

_____

_____

_____

Finances _____

_____

_____

_____

Fitness & Food _____

_____

_____

_____

Fun _____

_____

_____

_____

Flourish _____

_____

_____

_____

ex. 02.1

Setting my goodLife Goals

In his book "7 Habits of Highly Effective People," the renowned author, Stephen Covey, coined the phrase "start with the end in mind." To me, this is a brilliant piece of advice because only by knowing our destination first can we ascertain what we need to do next that can move us in that direction. Only by visualizing our dreamLife first can we know what we need to do as an interim "next step." The interim next step is specified in terms of goals that we set that if achieved will move us one step closer to our desired destination.

Now that you have dreamed big with no limits, it's time to distill those dreams into achievable and actionable goals to be accomplished over a specified period of time. Remember, your dreamLife is the life you wish to be living sometime in the distant future and it is the destination you work backwards from to create goals for the more immediate future (the next twelve months) that if attained, will put you one step closer to living your dream. Think of each year as another "interim step" towards manifesting the present dream into a present reality.

Where your dreamLife goals will be lofty and imprecise, your annual goals must be achievable, measurable and specific. You may be inclined to set a goal to "lose ten pounds," which is more specific than "slim down," but I suggest you be even more detailed. For example, explain exactly how you will lose the ten pounds: decide whether you will join a gym or hire a personal trainer, how many days per week you will work out, and if you're going to count calories in a journal or on a smart phone app.

And, beyond setting goals that are specific, attainable and measurable, it's important that you invest in some kind of accountability system – a friend, coach or tool – that can help keep you on track.

Although a "coach" is ideal, at the very least transfer your goals into an online goal-setting and accountability tool. There are many such goal-setting apps, tools or systems available for use. I'm often asked which is the best. My answer: "The best one is the one you will use."

Here are some examples in the six F-word categories to help you set your annual personal goals:

Faith
Example: Meditate each day. Pray daily. Attend a spiritual service once per week. Write down something each day that I am grateful for.

Family | Friends
Example: Tell my spouse/partner I love them every day. Call my daughter/sons/parents every day. Have a date-night with my spouse once per week. Have dinner with a friend once per month.

Finances
Example: Never spend money on my credit card that I can't pay in cash. Reconcile my budget every month. Pay off $_____ of debt. Buy one investment property.

Fitness | Food
Example: To lose ten pounds, work out with a trainer twice per week and walk three times per week. Limit my alcohol to 3 glasses of wine per week. Eliminate gluten from my diet. Get an acupuncture and massage once per month. Get a physical and all annual preventative exams.

Fun
Example: Golf twice per month. Take a painting class. Take a one-week staycation or a trip to Italy.

Flourish
Example: Read one business book per month. Attend two conferences; one business and one personal development. Learn at least one new technology.

Exercise 2.2: Setting my Annual goodLife Goals

The goal of this exercise is to set your goals for the calendar year.

Distill the dreamLife goals you created in the last exercise into specific goals you wish to achieve this year in each of the six life categories.

Afterwards, transfer those goals into an online goal-setting and accountability tool. Personally, I like an app called Everest. It can be downloaded from iTunes to your desktop/laptop, and integrates with your Smartphone and/or tablet.

Faith

Family | Friends

ex. 02.2

Finances

Fitness | Food

Fun

Flourish

ex. 02.2

Recap:

How does it feel to have established your dreamLife ambitions and goodLife goals for this year? How were the exercises? Did the reflection exercise at the beginning help you to better envision your dreamLife and add more clarity for this year's changes and goals? Are you ready to continue?

THOUGHTS & NOTES

ex. 02.2

THOUGHTS & NOTES

ex. 02.2

Chapter III

Step 3: Money Mapping My goodLife

"A budget is people telling their money where to go instead of wondering where it went."

John Maxwell

Now comes the fun stuff! Figuring you wouldn't be inclined to open a chapter about "budgeting," I created a new term: money mapping. Mapping your money is just a sexier way to say budgeting your money. If you're inclined to think that you don't need a budget, you're mistaken. A working budget is an essential element in the accumulation of wealth. The well-known money author, Dave Ramsey, explains it this way: "You have to make money behave, and a written plan (a budget) is the whip and chair for the money tamer!"

Despite the negative connotation associated with the word budget, the act of budgeting is actually quite enjoyable. In this chapter, I'll share with you how I make budgeting fun. No, it's not impossible! Let me give you an example: if you have never experienced an orgasm, you wouldn't know the pleasure you're missing, but once you know it, you want to experience it over and over. It's the same with budgeting, while consequently watching your money grow. It becomes addictive. It's that something else in life that you don't want to miss out on. (I told you I'd talk a little bit about sex!)

Before we get started talking about money, let me take a moment to discuss language. I'm not talking about proper grammar, punctuation or spelling, but about language in terms of how we use it to fulfill our intention of living a good life. Many of the definitions I offer in this manuscript are a hybrid—a blend of what you would see in the dictionary combined with my own explanation for how I actually use the word. I define words in a way that enables me to act with them. For example, a "money mapping" system makes more sense to me than a "budgeting system." Whether you agree with my practice of making up my own distinctions (and adopting the uncommon yet powerful ones of others), how we use language is vitally important. There is depth and beauty to language, yes, but more importantly, language is power. I admire and envy those who have a beautiful vocabulary and who always seem to have the perfect word to capture the true idea or essence of the moment.The concept of language is important in the context of this book because language is the most foundational element for designing our goodLife, an act that requires us to look at our every thought, observation, interpretation, and action. Do we know the meaning of the words we use? Are our definitions, interpretations, and understanding of the world around us our own as a matter of thoughtful choice? Or do we have only those that have been handed down from others?

As the famous author Don Miguel Ruiz says, "It is through our words that we manifest everything." In other words, if we don't like what we manifest in our life, we might take a look at our language —not only what we speak to others, but what we speak (think) to ourselves.

As you've probably guessed, I have invested time into the study of language. I believe that our linguistic distinctions equal our capacity for action and that there is a fundamental difference between "learning about" and "learning to do." We produce results with an ability to do, not an ability to know theoretically. Since the quality of my life largely depends on my ability to produce desired results, I give a lot of importance to linguistic distinctions; I embody them for the sake of designing and acting my life, not simply for the sake of knowing. And to keep me from falling into the trap of following the advice of others who "know," I have a rule: "Don't tell me you know something unless you've produced 7-figures."

Now let's talk about the language of budgeting. As a noun, the concept of budgeting is pretty simple to understand. The act of budgeting, as a verb, however, is more complex. And although many may "have" a budget, few actually engage in the "act" of budgeting. We may not be aware that the skill of budgeting treats the word budget as both a noun and a verb—we have a "budget" that we create and use as a tool to "budget." Make sense?

Budget as a noun refers to a money plan—a tool used to forecast and track future household income and expenses, debt-repayment and savings. As a verb, budget means to review and reconcile actual income and expenses against those forecasted. It also refers to working household monies for the sake of an improved financial situation.

My definition of the word as a noun allows me to use a budget as a plan and a tool; used as a verb, it tells me what to do in the act of budgeting. My practice (action) for budgeting starts by creating a budget (noun) and continues as a monthly commitment to budget (verb). In the remainder of this chapter we'll look at budget both as a noun and a verb.

Several methods and tools exist for creating and using a budget, some more helpful and effective than others. As part of my commitment towards wealth-building, I've examined a large number of budgeting techniques and tools to find a methodology that would enable me to fulfill my commitment. I found several that had great features, but they all seemed to be lacking in one way or another for my needs. So I took the best of them, meshed those together with my personal philosophy on money and wealth, and created my own budgeting technique. I will now share it with you.

My personal budgeting practice that I call my goodLife Money Mapping System consists of five parts, all of which I will describe in this chapter. In addition, I'll provide an exercise at the end of each part designed to help you put my philosophy into practice, the five parts are:

Part 1: Budgeting My goodLife ARMe
    Step 1: Planning for my Planned Expenses | Exercise 3.1
    Step 2: Planning for the Unplanned | Exercise 3.2

Part 2: Budgeting My Savings & Investments | Exercise 3.3

Part 3: Budgeting My Debt Payoff | Exercise 3.4

Part 4: Budgeting My goodLife's Little Luxuries | Exercise 3.5

Part 5: Budgeting My Income for Allocation | Exercise 3.6

Politically correct or not, I will say it: money is important and required to live a good life. Growing up poor, I know the ugly reality of living without money. One never forgets the pangs of hunger. But there is something worse than starvation: shame. I was a good kid. I surpassed expectations in school with straight-A averages; I excelled at sports and won numerous all-state awards; I was respected by my teachers, who considered me an exceptional student.

But even as a role model student and athlete, I carried an appalling secret. Utter desperation can spawn the unthinkable; in my case, my deprivation caused me to steal. I couldn't afford the basic essentials, so I lifted clothes, shoes, underwear, food-the necessities that required the money I didn't have. I hated myself for sinking so low. I eventually reached my breaking point and realized that stealing wasn't the answer. Making money was. I vowed to stop one and start the other. (An entrepreneur was born.)

But my vow to make money wasn't enough.

In my twenties and early thirties, I earned more in a year than my parents would earn in a lifetime. I accumulated the notorious big house, fancy cars, expensive vacations, and many other high-income luxuries. I had acquired the capacity for earning money but learned the hard way that the art of making money wasn't the secret to warding off poverty. I still didn't know how to keep my money. The result? After a divorce, bad investments and the IRS, I lost it all. I found myself in an all-too-familiar place: I was broke.

I lacked the means to cover my most basic expenses. Once, the day before my electricity was to be turned off, I was forced to ask friends for money to pay the bill. The experience humiliated and shamed me, but it was nothing compared to the deep sadness I felt for my children. My two beautiful, desperate children depended on me, now as a single mother, to provide for them, and I had so nearly failed. I resolved then and there that no way was I going to let them grow up like I had. I learned my bitter lesson, regrouped, and became determined to start again.

Starting over became a quest to learn not only the art of making money, but also the skill of keeping it. And yes, the keeping of money is a definite skill. In fact, the making of it is the easy part. The challenge with money is in knowing how to keep and grow it during your lifetime.

Since losing everything and starting over, I've studied under ambitious and smart rich people, attended numerous seminars, and read countless books on money and the skills for amassing wealth. What you are about to read in the following pages is the product of my learning. The philosophy, information, and practices I'm about to share with you are not derived from just one teacher or legacy—they are a fusion of accumulated knowledge acquired from the best teachers and mentors I've had the privilege of studying under for over a decade. All of these lessons start with one word: budgeting.

Today, my husband Garry and I are able to afford our goodLife thanks to our budgeting practices, but we are far from finished. We are still deep in the practices of earning, saving and investing until the time when our assets earn us more annual income than we generate from working. Working to earn an income high enough to support the lifestyle we desire is difficult. We can almost certainly count on a day when we will finally tire of all the effort. On that day, we will want our money to be able to do the hard work required to underwrite the cost of living our life.

Here's the great news: money can work much harder than we can. Money never gets sick, tired or disabled. It works twenty-four hours per day, three hundred sixty-five days per year. Knowing this, Garry and I are resolved to firmly master our money and make it work for us, covering the cost of our dreamLife so that we can live it, not just dream about it.

Other than our home mortgage and the loans for our ten investment properties (so far), we have zero consumer debt. We own a nice home in the wealthiest zip code in Austin. We own a 2013 Range Rover and a Lexus convertible that we paid for in cash, and our teenage children drive our paid-off hand-me-down cars—my old Infinity and Garry's old BMW (both with over 100,000 miles). We own the buildings where our goodLife offices are located, and we take a three-week European vacation each year that we pay for in-full and in cash. Over the years we have created many sources of income, and we have several million dollars of capital-at-work.

To add to our debt-free aspiration, our goal is to pay off our home mortgage as soon as possible. We have a fifteen-year note and systematically pay extra on our mortgage through automatic bi-monthly payments. This practice alone takes our note from a fifteen-year to a thirteen-point-five. In addition, we make one extra payment towards principal at the end of each calendar year, saving us approximately another eighteen months of payments. The bottom line? Our ritual will enable us to pay off our home mortgage in a little over ten years. Think of all of the money we'll be able to allocate to investing when our home mortgage money is no longer paid to the bank!

If you don't already have an automated bi-monthly mortgage payment, I recommend setting one up immediately. In fact, add that to your goal sheet right now. Simply paying your mortgage twice per month versus once will enable you to pay off your note quicker, freeing that money to be allocated elsewhere (hopefully into investments), and saving you thousands of dollars in additional interest. This process doesn't require additional money on your part; it simply prevents the balance on your loan from accruing another thirty days' worth of interest between payments. If you need help, call your local loan officer . A good one will become a valued member of your money management/investment team. If you don't have one, let me know and I will set you up with mine.

I share this story to prove that—despite growing up poor and going completely broke in my early thirties—I've been able to build wealth after only ten years of disciplined money habits and practices. If I could do this coming from my background, you can too. It just takes a little knowledge, earnest discipline and consistent budgeting practices. The truth is, it's easy to become wealthy if you understand and abide by the universal laws of money.

As mentioned above, my budgeting method consists of five parts reflected in the budget illustrated below. Let's begin by breaking down each part.

Part 1 | Budgeting My goodLife ARMe

Budgeting your ARMe consists of two steps:

Planning for my planned expenses
Planning for the unplanned

You begin the creation of your budget by establishing what I call your ARMe—the "Annual Minimum Required Expense" that your income must cover in order to stay afloat. A reality of life is that it costs to live, even at the most basic survival level. Survival expenses are required, whereas other expenses are not. Required expenses necessary to survive include the cost of housing, utilities, food, clothing, transportation and health care. On the other hand, cable, mani-pedis, and happy hours are not necessary.

Remember it this way: knowing this number enables you to keep your ARMe around your expenses. There are two categories of ARMe (required/necessary) reflected on your budget:

Required/Necessary Expenses Planned
Required/Necessary Expenses Unplanned

Planning for My Planned Expenses

The first category in your ARMe is "Planned Expenses"—that is, necessary expenses for which you can plan and itemize on your budget. Planned expenses usually show up as recurring payments made on a monthly, quarterly, or semi-annual basis. They can be planned for because they occur regularly and are therefore predictable.

To accumulate wealth, it's imperative that you differentiate your ARMe from other expenses in your budget. Keep a focus on the minimum amount required to run your household and exclude extraneous expenses (we'll talk about those later). Below are examples to help categorize your spending.

Examples of Planned ARMe:
- Mortgage or rent payment (you must have a place to live)
- Groceries (you must eat)
- Utilities (you must keep the lights on and the water running)
- Clothing (you must have protection from the elements)
- Car payment, insurance and gas (you must be able to get from point A to point B)
- Health insurance/prescriptions (you must take care of your health)

Examples of Unplanned ARMe:
- New water heater
- Insurance deductible
- Snow-storm damage

Examples of non-ARMe (not required) expenses that likely show up on your budget with your ARMe when they shouldn't:
- Clothing
  - Some clothing is required and will therefore be allocated as an ARMe expense. Kids, for example, grow out of clothes and need new ones.

    - Other clothing is not required and will therefore be allo-
cated as a non-ARMe expense. You know that your fourth
pair of black boots probably isn't completely necessary.

- Big screen TV payment
- Premium cable bill
- Restaurant bills

Exercise 3.1: Planning for My Planned Expenses

To complete this exercise, you'll need the following tools:
- An itemized list of all your expenses from last year
- All household bills and expenses (mortgage, car loan, utilities, etc.) from last year
- All monthly bank statements from last year
- All credit card statements from last year
- Red and blue highlighters (real or virtual)
- An accounting program

[pro tips]

Mint is an excellent, simple-to-use program to manage household (and self-employed) finances

QuickBooks is for those who own an LLC or corporation, invoice clients online, maintain a merchant account, have payroll, and/or need full tax reporting capabilities.

Instructions:

1. Using the resources listed above, reconcile all statements from last year. Reconciling is like the old days of "balancing your checkbook." It means breaking down each charge on your credit cards and assigning each charge to an appropriate expense.

2. Find and calculate the annual expense of the following ARMe from last year:

Household

Mortgage/rent	$_____
(PITI: Principle, interest, taxes and insurance)	
Utilities	$_____
Pest Control	$_____
Phone	$_____
Groceries/Food	$_____

ex. 03.1

Clothing Purchases $_____
Dry Cleaning $_____
Children's Clothing $_____
Auto expenses $_____
Self-Care/Health Care $_____
Kids school/activities $_____
Play/Hobbies $_____
Other $_____
(be specific and categorize if necessary

3. Create an ARMe chart of accounts that matches the illustration below, using the budgeting software of choice. Then place your actual expenses (taken from the blanks you fille in above) into the respective chart of accounts [see figure 2].

4. Once you've added all expenses into the appropriate chart of accounts, re-assess each expense:
    •   Make sure that all expenses in this ARMe section are in fact required expenses (necessary)
    •   Highlight any non-required expenses (unnecessary) with a red highlighter
    •   Highlight any surprise expenses (unplanned) with a blue highlighter

5. Review this ARMe once more, and then remove any red or blue highlights. Keep note of them, however, because you will later add them back into a different section of your budget.

The sum you have at this point is your Planned Annual Required Minimum Expense for your household—the required cost of operating your household. In other words, this number represents the minimum amount of income you must earn to cover your most basic living expenses (assuming no unplanned surprise expenses). If your income does not cover your ARMe, you will be required to lower

ex. 03.1

these expenses in one way or another. For example, you may have to downsize your house/rent payment or sell a car.

planned ARMe EXPENSES (pA)	
Household and Family	
Mortgage/Rent	
Property Taxes	
Property Insurance	
Utilities	
Pest Control	
Mobile Phone	
Groceries/Food	
Clothing	
Kids Clothing	
Dry Cleaning	
Total Household and Family	$ -
Auto	
Car Payment	
Fuel	
Maintenance	
Auto Insurance	
Total Auto	$ -
Self Care	
Health Insurance	
Medicine	
Co-Pays	
Massage	
Chiropractor	
Massage	
Acupuncture	
Chiropractor	
Gym|Trainer	
Yoga	
Barber|Salon	
Total Self-Care	$ -
Kids School/Activities	$ -
Play/Hobbies	$ -
TOTAL planned ARMe EXPENSES (pA)	$ -

[figure 2] **Planned ARMe Chart of Accounts**

ex. 03.1

Planning for the Unplanned

We've covered the planned ARMe category. Now, we will discuss the second ARMe category as the second part of budgeting—what I call "planning for the unplanned." The sum of these two ARMe categories represents the absolute minimum amount of income you must earn to cover your most basic living expenses.

Many people who create an annual budget and work to live within their means often continue to find themselves in the red at the end of each year. Why? Because they didn't budget for unplanned expenses. To prevent this happening to you, it's essential to plan for the unplanned.

What are unplanned expenses? As the name implies, they're expenses that drop in our lap when we don't expect them. A story I like to share involves one of my team members, Scotty. A couple of years ago he was horsing around and playfully jumped over a coffee table. He didn't quite make the jump and crashed to the floor. The next day, at the doctor's office, Scotty learned that he had torn his ACL and would need surgery.

The good news is that, as an independent contractor, he had health insurance that covered the cost of surgery; his recurring insurance ex-pense was entered as a planned expense on his budget. The bad news is that his insurance plan included a $2,000 deductible, which Scotty had not planned for and did not have money to cover. As a result, he put the $2,000 charge on his credit card, plunging him into debt that he hadn't expected and didn't want.

Think about these stats: 75% of Americans say that they would borrow on a credit card if a rainy day came; 49% could cover less than one month's expenses if they lost their income.

Scotty fit into the 75% statistic. When his rainy day arrived, he was forced into debt and borrowed on a credit card. This not only hurt his financial situation, but also his mental health. He reported to me that this setback caused him anxiety and depression. He felt that he was just getting ahead and then—Bam!—he was in the hole again. He also said the situation created tension in his relationship and caused a huge fight about money.

To avoid being one of these American statistics, Garry and I plan for the unplanned. We set aside money for a rainy day, and we don't touch that money unless we find ourselves in an unplanned situation. For ex-ample, last year our pool pump met the end of its lifecycle. The expense to replace the equipment was unplanned, as we had no way of knowing it would break. However, the expense didn't throw us off budget because we had planned for an unexpected situation like this one.

Planning for the unplanned requires three disciplines:

Save up to the maximum amount you deem necessary to cover unplanned expenses.

Sweep monthly income into a savings account until the maximum amount is saved.

When all or part of the savings is used to cover unplanned expenditures, resume sweeping monthly income into the savings account to replenish the gap.

As part of our practice, Garry and I have an "Unplanned Expense Savings Account" in which we accumulate the maximum amount we deem necessary to cover unplanned expenses in any given year. The list below shows the actual unplanned expense categories this account covers when needed.

Auto   Medical   Household   Emergencies   Other

Auto Deductibles and Repairs

Garry and I don't have a car payment expense because our cars are paid off, but if you have one or more car payments, they go in the Planned Expense budget. Your insurance expense should also be included in the Planned expense section.

Even though we own our cars, we are obligated to carry insurance. While the insurance premium is accounted for in our Planned Expenses, the deductible is not. A deductible is an Unplanned ARMe (Required); you can't plan ahead for when you may need to expense it, and you're re-quired to cover the deductible if you find yourself in an at-fault accident. Therefore, you want to ensure that the deductible is covered in your budget.

The same goes for auto repairs. For example, three of our cars no longer have warranties, and because they are older cars it's likely they'll require some repair. We don't exactly know what or when the repairs might be necessary, but we have money saved just in case. This came in handy when my daughter's A/C went out in the middle of our Texas summer. We have the total of our deductibles and estimated repairs saved in our Unplanned Expense Savings Account.

Medical Deductibles and Uncovered Expenses

Medical expenses work similarly to auto expenses. Health insurance premiums and monthly prescriptions/supplements are part of your Planned Expense budget. Co-Pays and deductibles are part of the Un-planned Expense budget.

This can be rather simple if you're employed by a company that offers insurance, but it can be a little tricky if you are not covered under an employer policy. That's often the case for entrepreneurs and small business owners.

Garry and I have a Health Savings Account with a $5,000 per-individual deductible. After meeting the deductible, we are 100%

covered (with an asterisk, of course!). While our health insurance premium is a Planned Expense, the $10,000 deductible is an Unplanned Expense. We pay all doctors' bills, prescriptions and co-pays fully out of pocket, but each of the personally paid medical bills counts against our deductible. This means that the maximum cost of our covered health care is $10,000 per year, which would assume a sizable medical expense. This might come into play if a member of our family needed surgery or costly exams.

So, how much do we have saved for unplanned medical expenses?

Yes, we have the $10,000, but that is not all. Many of our healthcare costs are not covered by insurance and are not part of our deductible. We pre-fer functional medicine doctors, many of whom do not accept insurance. In addition, much of our healthcare cost fits in the preventative/self-care category comprised of expenses associated with acupuncture, chiropractic, nutrition, dental, therapy, gym/exercise and massage. I view my health as my most important asset and therefore spend accordingly.

Garry and I started by allocating 5% of our income to healthcare. We save the allocation in our Unplanned Saving Account.

Household Deductibles and Repairs
Home insurance premiums are accounted for in the Planned Expense budget. The amount of the household insurance deductible is an Unplanned Expense.

In addition, unexpected home repairs not covered by insurance can often catch us offguard if we don't budget for them. Repairs are not the same as home improvements. Repairs are classified as Required Expenses and are part of your ARMe. Home improvements are in a different category. While upgrading the appliances would be considered a home improvement in our household, replacing the broken dishwasher would be an Unplanned Required Expense.

We have the combined total of our household deductible and estimated repairs saved in our Unplanned Expense Savings Account.

Emergencies

Different types of insurance exist to deal with catastrophes. Garry and I each carry disability Insurance *and* life Insurance, and I highly recommend both. It's more likely that you will be disabled than die unexpectedly, so disability insurance can cover your household expenses in the event that you cannot earn an income due to serious injury. And in my opinion, anyone with a family (spouse/partner and/or children) should maintain life insurance as a basic adult responsibility. If you do not carry both of these, I recommend you talk with your financial planner or insurance agent.

After reaching a certain net worth, I also recommend carrying an umbrella policy. Again, your financial advisor or insurance agent can advise you about coverage to suit your particular situation. Sometimes life happens, but by planning for the unplanned and carrying adequate insurance (and staying out of debt), you can avoid unexpectedly finding yourself in a horrible financial situation.

Estimating for emergencies is a judgment call. Garry and I have insurance to cover emergencies. If you do not, you probably want to allocate money here [see figure 3].

unplanned ARMe EXPENSES (uA)	
Automobile Deductibles	
Automobile Repairs	
Medical Insurance Deductibles	
Medical Uncovered Expenses	
Household Insurance Deductibles	
Household Repairs	
Emergencies	
TOTAL unplanned ARMe EXPENSES (uA)	$ -

[figure 3] Unplanned ARMe Chart of Accounts

Exercise 3.2: Planning for the Unplanned

Once you've completed the last exercise, you will have established your Planned ARMe based on last year's actual expenses. Those numbers should now be recorded in your budgeting software, organized into a Planned ARMe chart of accounts.

But you're not yet finished calculating your ARMe. You'll now want to plan for the unplanned by forecasting potential surprise expenses that could hit your budget unexpectedly. When you complete this exercise, you'll know the total annual required minimum amount needed to operate your household. As an assist, think of the formula like this:

Required/Necessary Expenses (Planned) + Required/Necessary Expenses (Unplanned) = ARMe

To get started, fill in these blanks:
- Re-assess and re-calculate your planned expenses ARMe:
  $_____

- Determine your unplanned expenses total. This will be the sum of the four parts described above, plus any other categorical expense you consider unplanned:

- Auto deductible, repairs, other auto unplanned:
  $_____ $_____
  $_____

- Medical deductible/co-pays, uncovered expenses, other medical unplanned:
  $_____ $_____
  $_____

ex. 03.2

- Household deductible, repairs, other household unplanned:

  $_____ $_____

  $_____

- Determine your strategy of planning for emergencies/catastrophes (e.g., unexpected death, including death expenses to surviving spouse, disability, lawsuit)

[pro tip]

Add actionable goals to your goal sheet

For example: find a competent financial/estate planner/attorney, obtain life insurance, obtain disability insurance

What is your planned expense ARMe? If you don't know it off the top of your head, find it now

Tools:
- Calculator
- Twelve Bank Statements for the calendar year (last year)
- Twelve Credit Card Statements for the calendar year (last year)
- Insurance policies (auto, health, household)

Instructions:
1. Review your actual expenses from the last calendar year and identify which expenses were unexpected and unplanned.
   - You should have highlighted those in blue in the last assignment.
   - If you added all your annual expenses in the "planned section" in the last assignment, you should now move those that you categorized as unplanned to the unplanned section. Remember, these are usually non-recurring expenses like a one-time a/c or heater replacement.

ex. 03.2

2. Add/Move unplanned annual expenses into their respective categories in the Unplanned ARMe section of your budget.

3. Note the deductible amounts on your different insurance policies; add the deductibles to the respective section.

4. Assess the amounts in each category: does this seem like an adequate amount? Adjust if necessary.

5. Double-check to make sure you moved all unplanned expenses out of the planned expense section. It's important that you don't double-enter any expenses.

ex. 03.2

THOUGHTS & NOTES

_____
_____
_____
_____
_____
_____
_____
_____
_____
_____
_____
_____
_____
_____
_____
_____
_____
_____
_____
_____
_____
_____
_____
_____

ex. 03.2

Part 2 | Budgeting for my Savings & Investments

> "Most people spend more time picking out a suit than planning their careers and retirement."
>
> *Earl Nightingale*

We have now distinguished between ARMe and non-ARMe expenses, and also included budgeting for unplanned expenses that can throw us off our budget. Keep in mind that few people know their minimum number—a key reason they spend too much and, consequently, don't have enough money to save and invest.

Because most people don't separate their required expenses from those not required (I discuss these "little luxuries" in Part 4), they use up their entire monthly paycheck on expenses before they save or invest a single dollar. This irresponsible money practice is why 97% of seniors don't have enough savings and investments to live a goodLife when they retire. Yes, that's 97%! I don't want you to be lumped into that statistic.

Before we start, let me ask a few questions: Answer with a yes or no.

- Do you have sufficient savings?
- Do you plan your savings?
- Do you systematically save for your investments?
- Are you planning for your retirement?

Those who know me are aware that I am dedicated to taking care of my health. I eat high-quality organic gluten-free foods; I limit my intake of sugar, caffeine and alcohol; I exercise regularly, and I weigh the same as I did in high school. As a result, I have rarely needed to see a doctor.

However, in early 2013 I unexpectedly became sick—very sick. So sick, in fact, that I was incapacitated and unable to work for six months. Garry could barely work because he became my full-time caretaker. Our life went from great to a living hell practically overnight. Instead of going to the office every day, our days were filled with doctor's appointments, IVs, phone calls, and obsessive internet searches. Each day I awoke hoping to feel better, only to feel worse.

After four months of searching for what was wrong, I was finally diagnosed. The ensuing two months were dedicated to full-time treatment with hopes, but no guarantee, of recovery. The bad news is that I accrued just shy of $200,000 worth of uncovered medical bills. But because of these budgeting practices I'm sharing with you, Garry and I were able to pay those bills in cash—without going into debt and without liquidating any assets.

To get us started in this section, I'll offer a vocabulary lesson covering some of my favorite words. You may think you know these words, but bear with me—I'm betting you'll want to readjust your definitions somewhat! The terms I'm referring to are: savings, investments, compound interest, assets, and net worth.

Savings and investments are similar in that they refer to money intended for future purposes. However, they're not interchangeable. The small percentage of people who do save often think they're doing enough—but savings alone cannot provide you with a future goodLife. The following is the way I distinguish between savings and investments.

Savings:
- Savings are for a future in the short-term
- Savings usually sit in a bank account, earning only a small rate of interest

- Savings are liquid, meaning you can easily access and use them without penalty

Investments:
- Investments are for a future in the long-term—usually for retirement
- Investments are capital-at-work that tend to produce higher rates of return and compound over time
- Investments are not liquid and therefore are difficult and costly to liquidate

Savings cannot substitute for investments because savings accounts usually accrue simple interest, while investments more commonly earn compound interest. Compounding, or compound interest, is the ability of an asset to generate earnings, which are then reinvested to generate their own earnings. In other words, compounding refers to generating earnings from previous earnings.

Albert Einstein referred to compound interest as the eighth wonder of the world. I agree with him: if you can harness its power, compound interest can completely change your financial status over time. For example, according to a 2012 survey conducted by American Express, the average American family of four spends nearly $5,000 on a typical summer vacation. If that family invested that $5,000 at a 20% rate of return, they would amass around $476,000 in twenty-five years—and that's without adding additional money to the investment. Imagine what your bank accounts would look like if you allocated just some of the funds for your large expenditures towards investments instead [see figure 4].

Next, I wish you to re-learn the definition of "asset." Most of us think in accounting terms when we hear that word. I once did! Thanks to my accounting degree, I considered an asset to be an item listed on a balance sheet that represented something owned. But that definition is actually counter-productive to personal

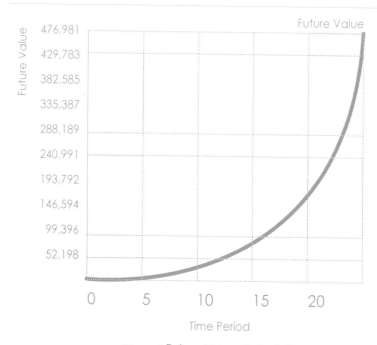

[figure 4] Future Value Calculation

wealth-building. Here is how you can think of assets from now on: assets are money used to create more money.

This distinction puts an end to considering the value of your car and the equity in your homestead to be an asset. The depreciating value of your car excludes it from being calculated as part of your net worth, and home equity can't be counted because that money can't be used to make more money. Assets, according to my definition, are only those things that contribute to our long-term net worth and help us become wealthy.

The words "net worth" and "wealth" can be used interchangeably. The accounting definition is the sum of your assets minus your liabilities. However, to make it useful for me (and you), I think of the value of net worth in terms of income, not assets or liabilities.

According to my distinction, net worth is the amount of money (income-producing assets) I have that I could live on if I lost my working income. Assuming a conservative 4% withdrawal of funds (net worth) at a said future withdrawal date, I consider every $1 of net worth on my balance sheet to be worth $4 of income at retirement. Every multiple of $4k that I need to support the cost of my living in retirement requires another $1 million of net worth. Looking at my balance sheet this way, rather than my CPA's way, enables me to better understand my true financial situation and act accordingly.

Early on we established that, if we're to get where we're going, we need to know where we are. For that reason we began by reflecting on our current situation before setting future goals. This same notion applies when contemplating our net worth. Reflecting on our current net worth requires that we ask the following questions:

- How much annual income do your assets produce?
- Could you live off that income if you lost your working income today?
- What income will you live off of when you retire if you don't have enough net worth?

My dreamLife requires that I have enough net worth to be "wealthy," which I associate with financial freedom. I will be financially free when the income produced from my net worth covers the cost of living my dreamLife. In every exchange with my balance sheet, I carry on this conversation with myself: "Is my net worth enough to cover all of my expenses? No? Then I'm not wealthy yet. Keep working, saving, and investing." A chance exists that I won't achieve full financial freedom, but it's not an option that my wealth not cover the cost of living my goodLife. This promise to myself is what keeps me on track with my spending, saving and investing.

I used the phrase "high-income poor person" earlier in the book. It's a concept I am familiar with because, at one time, I embodied that phrase. I made a healthy six-figure income and owned lots of toys, but I also had lofty debt and virtually no compounding assets. Had I calculated my net worth at the time, it would have shocked me to

Assets		
Personal Items		
Vehicles	$	-
Jewelry	$	-
Other	$	-
Cash or Cash Equivalent		
Checking Account	$	-
Savings Accounts	$	-
Certificates of Deposit	$	-
Money Market Account	$	-
Life Insurance (cash value)	$	-
Business Checking Account	$	-
Other	$	-
Investments		
Retirement Account	$	-
Bonds	$	-
Mutual Funds	$	-
Stocks	$	-
Real Estate	$	-
Other	$	-
Total Assets	$	-
Liabilities		
Loan Balances		
Home Equity Loan	$	-
Car Loans	$	-
Real Estate Loans	$	-
Student Loans	$	-
Loans on Life Insuance	$	-
Income Taxes Payable	$	-
Other Outstanding Debt		
Credit Card Debt	$	-
Other Debt	$	-
Total Liabilities	$	-
Estimated Net Worth	$	-

[figure 5] Net Worth Statement

ex. 01

learn that I was worth less than zero—that I owed more to the banks than I owned, showing my net worth to be in the red. I even venture to say that I was worse off than I had been in childhood. Why? Because my parents couldn't afford debt, leaving our net worth, at its worst, at zero [see figure 5].

Having a net worth of zero (or below) is a seriously risky financial situation to be in, but certainly not uncommon. We live in a culture of consumption and immediate gratification in which 90% of Americans regularly make purchases they can't afford. But the root of the problem lies even deeper than this foolishness: the source is our own ignorance. We were not taught in school the skills to manage money, and for most of us neither our parents nor peers are good examples of financial prudence.

As part of our practice, Garry and I first put money aside for saving and investing; then we budget for spending that is outside of our ARMe (necessary household expenses). Now, if you're really good at monitoring your money and staying on top of your finances, you may choose to use only one large savings account, which will potentially earn more interest than separate accounts. However, if you're not that organized and will be frequently moving around the money in these accounts, then the minimal interest may not be worth the hassle.

Garry and I find it easier to use the multiple accounts technique. In addition to the Unplanned Expense Savings account that I mentioned previously, we have six savings accounts, and we allocate money to them in this order:

Tax Holding Account

This really isn't a savings account, but more of a holding account. Our income is comprised of both salary and 1099/K1 income. Like everyone else who is on salary, our employer (goodLife Companies) collects the taxes before we receive our check. For our 099 income, however, we receive the amount in full but are responsible for paying taxes ourselves. Since a big chunk of this money doesn't belong to us, but to Uncle Sam, we created our Tax Holding Account; it's where we shave a portion of all 1099/K1 income to cover taxes due when the time comes to pay them.

Six Months' Reserves Savings Account (required savings)

A reserve account is for monies saved to cover the cost of your household expenses in the event of temporary loss of income. For a business owner, going without an income for a period of time isn't implausible. For those employed, there is always a chance of being laid off or fired.

Garry and I save six months of our ARMe as reserves. We only save ARMe expenses and not total expenses because we can always eliminate the non-ARMe expenses if necessary. In the case of my personal health crisis, I was grateful to have had reserves. We had enough stress dealing with the illness itself; I couldn't imagine if I had to worry about money as well!

Investment Savings Account (required savings)

An investment account is for monies saved that will eventually be invested. Investing is a learned skill, and I advise you to "invest" in your own education about the subject. Never relinquish your money to third parties! They will never care for your money like you do. Have you noticed that you may have lost money on your stock investments for the year, but your stockbroker still collected his fees? Who else gets to collect money for underperformance?

Another tip is to automate your investing as much as possible. David Bach calls this practice "paying yourself first." For example, if you wish to contribute a designated amount of your paycheck to investing into an Index Fund, you can set it up to auto-draft from your bank account each month. If the money is shaved off the top of your income, you can't spend it! Uncle Sam gets his money first, why not you?

The rule of thumb is to invest 15% of your income. Garry and I earmark 17% of our combined (gross) household income for investments. Most of our investments are in real estate holdings, but we also invest in Vanguard Index Funds. We do not use traditional stock brokers or investment managers. In our experience, they provide lower returns than Index Funds once we factor their fees (disclosed and undisclosed) into our overall return.

To learn more about this type of passive investing, I recommend a book suggested to me by one of my mentors: "Unconventional Success," by David Swensen. It's not easy reading, but absolutely worth it if you wish to better understand stock investments.

College Savings Account (required savings)

A college savings account holds monies saved for kids' college education, assuming you are not investing in any other specific college fund. Believe it or not, 65% of Americans have saved nothing towards their child's college education. That's why, in 2013, total student federal loan debt topped $1 trillion—a figure that doesn't include the additional debt parents have taken on to help pay for their children's education. The average student borrower graduates $26,600 in the red and one in ten graduates will accumulate more than $40,000 in debt. Talk about foolish.

Had we started sooner, Garry and I would have put money into a compounding investment college fund when the kids were young. Because we were way late to the game, we are simply saving for the future expenses. Garry and I have two children, and both are approaching college age. We expect their combined educations to cost us $50,000 per year. This means we must save approximately $200,000.

Vacation Savings Account (luxury savings)

Yes, Garry and I even save for our vacations. We plan our vacation one year before we take it. We save the total estimated cost of the vacation, including travel, tips, and spending cash. In the beginning of our marriage, we saved for nice staycations. Most recently we enjoyed a luxurious three week vacation through Eastern Europe completely paid for out of our vacation savings.

Large Luxury Purchases Savings Account (luxury savings)

A large luxury account is a place to accumulate money that can be used for costly purchases that might otherwise require debt or dipping into savings. Examples of large purchases include cars, household improvements, and Christmas presents. The practice of saving for large purchases is the secret to staying out of debt (well, when combined with resisting the impulse of immediate gratification!).

Because Garry and I are committed to living a lifestyle we can afford, we have pledged to live a life free of personal debt. For this reason, we don't maintain balances on credit cards; instead, we pay for large purchases in cash (for example, we saved for two years before buying our last car). We are equally committed to saving and investing as much as possible. Therefore, we make the most of those large purchases: two of our cars have over 100,000 miles and may have another 100,000 miles to go before we replace them.

You may think our practice is absurd. I do not argue otherwise. As opposed to what some may think, there is no one way, best way, or only way to accumulate wealth. If my method and practice don't work for you, I will spend no time trying to convince you that it should. The only thing you will hear me advocate is any method that enables you to obtain financial freedom—a lifestyle free of debt that offers the ability to build adequate savings and investments. This is the only way to live a goodLife today and in the future.

I also have two tips for you to keep in mind as you embark on your wealth-building plan, whatever it may be.

First, start responsible money-management practices while still young. If I could do anything over again, I would start this practice earlier in my life. If I had, I would be far more financially secure than I am today.

Second, instead of thinking in terms of "money saved," think of "money invested." How much could that dollar saved be worth if invested in a compounding asset? Before I understood the impact of compound interest, I valued buying something on sale because it saved me money right then. Now, however, I know that buying sale items saves me money now and will earn me money in the future when I invest my savings.

Perhaps you're thinking that this module doesn't apply to you. Maybe, for example, you plan to never retire. Regardless, lack of savings and investments is an American epidemic that will affect you if you don't take action. How do you know you'll be able to work until you die? What if you become sick or disabled? What's the likelihood that you will want to work as hard when you're a senior as you do today? Wouldn't you like to play a little more golf or spend more time with the grandkids? The hard truth is that Social Security won't support much of a lifestyle, and if you don't have income-producing assets at retirement, Social Security is all you *will* have.

Here are a few statistics to consider: 28% of American families have no savings, and only 43% have enough to cover three months worth of expenses. Ninety-seven out of one hundred seniors lack the re-sources to write a check for $600. If these people had become sick like I did, many would not have been able to bounce back. Don't let that happen to you [see figure 6].

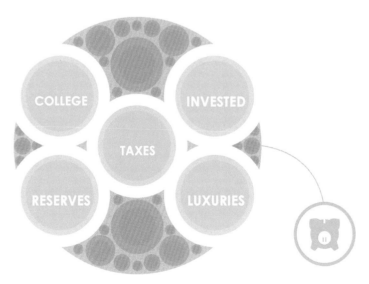

[figure 6] Savings Account Visual Aid

Exercise 3.3:
Budgeting for My Savings and Investments

At the completion of the last exercise, you calculated your ARMe by budgeting for your required planned and unplanned expenses. You now know the approximate minimum cost of operating your household.

In this exercise you'll plan for this year's saving and investing. With the help of a compounding table you will determine what your investment capital-at-work today will be worth in the future. This figure [see Appendix] will help you determine how much to invest annually to reach a net worth you can retire on. These are loose figures to help get you started on the journey to saving and investing. I recommend that you talk to your financial planner to determine your true investment strategy.

Tools:
- Calculator
- Statements showing current balances for your Savings Accounts
- Investment Statements showing balances for your 401k plans, Stock/Mutual Funds, equity in real estate holdings, and college funds
- Insurance Policies

To get started, fill in these blanks:
Savings:
1. How much do you have saved, not including investments?

   $_____

2. This year, how much additional money do you wish to save for:
   - Unplanned Expenses? $_____
   - Home Reserve? $_____

ex. 03.3

Consider how many months' ARMe you wish to cover if loss of income occurs

- Vacation(s): $_____
- Large Purchases/Home Improvements?

  $_____
- Large Future Purchases (e.g. a car) or reserves this year?

  $_____
- College/Other? $_____

  I recommend you talk to a financial advisor to find th best program/solution for your family. My only advice here: start when your children are born.

3. Calculate the total amount you wish to save this year:

   $_____

Investments:

4. Using a compounding table and your investment account information, answer the following questions [see Appendix]:
   - How much do you have invested today for retirement?

     $_____
   - What is the average annual return you expect from your investments? $_____

     [If you don't know, a rule of thumb is 8%.]
   - How many years from today do you plan to retire?

     _____
   - How much will your current investments be worth when you retire? $_____
   - How much money do you need for retirement?

     $_____

   I use this rule of thumb: multiply the annual income you wish to have at retirement x25. For example, if you wish to live off $100,000 at retirement, multiply that by 25. $100,000 x 25 = $2,500,000 invested at retirement.

ex. 03.3

5. Calculate your Investment Savings Number:

$\$$_____

- This is the amount you must invest annually in order to accumulate the necessary capital-at-work to produce income to fund your retirement lifestyle.
- Use the average annual return (minus fees) you get on your investments now.
- A rule of thumb is 8%.
- Make sure to take into account the amount you already have invested.

6. Transfer the calculated numbers above into the respective cells on your budget [see figure 7].

7. Assess the amount in each category, and adjust if necessary.

[pro tip]
It's likely that the amount of your Investment Savings Number is frightfully high. Don't panic! This number is intended to shock you. My goal is to trigger you to take action. If your Investment Savings Number is too high and therefore unrealistic, replace it with any number that you promise to save and invest this year. Anything is better than nothing.

Remember: Compound interest makes you rich, but it takes discipline and time to work. Unless you are willing to live without many of life's little luxuries today, you will likely procrastinate with your investing—and thereby thwart your chance to become rich.

If you complete this exercise, you will be in the 5% of Americans who do this level of money planning.

ex. 03.3

SAVING AND investing (Si)
1099 Taxes
Auto-Withdrawal into Investment
6-Months ARMe Savings
Investment Savings
Vacation Savings
Dream Savings (Car, Home Improvement)
TOTAL SAVING AND investing (Si) $ -

[figure 7] Savings and Investing

Recap:

Congrats! You now have a plan for how much you must save and invest next year BEFORE you spend money on those little luxuries. You're closer to not only living your goodLife today, but also securing a goodLife for your future.

After completing this exercise, did you notice that you've been living a life you can't afford? Have you been indulging on life's little luxuries before saving and investing? What are your thoughts now about saving and investing? Did this exercise provoke any new thinking?

How do you feel? Happy? Sad? Overwhelmed and uncomfortable? If you feel happy, you've likely discovered that you're on track for the goodLife and feel good about that. If you're sad, it's likely that you feel you're behind or not on track. That's great, because it means the work you've done so far can trigger you to change bad habits and practices that may be thwarting your intentions to live a goodLife. If you are overwhelmed, that means you are learning something new that can change your life. Learning is uncomfortable, which is why most people stop putting in the effort.

So, no matter what you are feeling right now, I congratulate you for taking a step in the right direction!

ex. 03.3

THOUGHTS & NOTES

ex. 03.3

Part 3 | Budgeting My Debt Payoff

"A man in debt is so far a slave."

Ralph Waldo Emerson

If you hadn't already, I hope you now realize the importance of saving and investing, and that it must come before spending money on anything (aside from your ARMe). This life practice takes both commitment and discipline, because we live in a culture of "you want it, you buy it"—a behavior guaranteed to lead to a discussion of debt payoff.

Part 3 of budgeting attacks debt. If you are one of the small percentages of people who don't have debt, feel free to skip Part 3. However, you may find the advice here to be useful in helping others steer clear of indebted slavery to banks and creditors. For that reason, I encourage you to read Part 3 even if you're personally debt-free.

The first section of "Budgeting for My Debt Payoff" deals with redefining debt and discusses how to prevent accumulating more of it. The second section addresses an actual plan for resolving the debt you may currently possess.

Before my own financial enlightenment (triggered by going broke in my early thirties), I had no understanding of the principles of money. Perhaps it's because I only graduated with a B average and not an A. However, despite a dual business degree in accounting and finance, I entered the real world with no true understanding of three important financial terms: money, debt, and compound interest. I could easily recite the accounting definitions of assets, liabilities, and depreciation, and I could build excellent business financial spreadsheets. But I had acquired no knowledge of how these financial terms applied to my real life. It never occurred to me that business and household finances are cut from the same cloth: the financial prudence required to run a healthy business is equally necessary to operate a financially healthy household.

As a result, I quickly became the American statistic—I enjoyed living a life I couldn't afford. Not only did I spend all of my high six-figure income, I also acquired debt while doing so. The bank owned my life. After paying my many expenses, my monthly earnings netted out at zero each month. I had the monthly mortgage on a big house in the suburbs, the monthly payments on fancy new cars, and the credit card bills acquired from the latest luxury ski vacation. I paid for my children's nannies and private school tuitions. I employed maids, landscapers, and pool cleaners to keep the house and toys in mint condition.

I thought I was living the American dream. Sadly, I was living the American nightmare. It still pains me to think how much more I would be worth today had I chosen to live a life I could afford and invested seriously instead of spending frivolously.

In my mind, money mastery is an applied science that we all need to learn regardless of education, age, race, or gender. We should be taught money in elementary school alongside the basics of reading and arithmetic. If we were, perhaps our entire country would boast financial health statistics flipped from the current numbers. But since we are not, we must take responsibility for mastering money as adults.

Our lack of concern for debt as a culture is alarming. Debt has become such a prevalent and accepted part of the American Way that we can't imagine having a home without a mortgage, a car without a car payment, college without a student loan, or a credit card without a balance.

I have three questions for you:

Including your home, cars, education and credit cards, how much total debt do you have?

$_____

What is the total monthly expenditure going towards these debt payoffs?

$_____

Assuming an 8% return, how much would you be worth in twenty-five years if you allocated the sum of the two previous questions to investments instead of towards the cost of borrowing?

$_____

The answer to the final question will seem unbelievable, but I assure you it's feasible. Now, I wish to challenge many other mindsets that I think could be thwarting your ability to become financially independent. Some of these mindsets will prove stubborn to dislodge, so I'll provide you with my cardinal rules for becoming wealthy. They apply to the four most common forms of personal debt: home mortgages, car loans, credit card balances, and student loan debt.

Home Mortgage

Because of the size of the loan required to purchase a home, a very small percentage of Americans can pay cash for their homestead. Home ownership has many benefits, and having to take out a mortgage should not necessarily prevent you from buying a home. However, it's important to evolve our way of thinking about this investment.

Notice the word "investment." It's common for homeowners to refer to their property in this way, but I have a somewhat radical claim to make against this term. Ready for it? The value and/or equity in your home doesn't matter.

The rules are a little different for investment and rental properties, but overall, the "investment" in your home isn't the equity, contrary to common belief. Sure, equity matters if you intend to sell the property or leave it to your kids as part of your estate, but otherwise it does not matter at all. The "investment" part of your home is actually the eventual opportunity to live debt-free. Being free of a home mortgage offers two advantages:

1. The opportunity to repurpose the money going towards our largest monthly expense, transforming it into our largest monthly deposit into investments.
2. The opportunity to live our retirement years without rent by owning our home free and clear. Our homestead, in this case, becomes part of our retirement strategy.

At this point, I need to remind you that I am not a financial advisor and am not qualified to offer you financial advice. I know that my beliefs are contrary to the way many think and may therefore be controversial. However, I believe that my personal experience and my extensive study of the practices of rich people can offer a lot of value.

In particular, I believe that I have a lot of knowledge to offer about mortgage debt because real estate is my business. I feel strongly that the definition of "home investment," along with two other misconceptions about mortgage financing, comprise major barriers to the accumulation of wealth. In fact, these misconceptions were a major factor in the housing bubble that burst in 2007. To keep you from making those same mistakes, let me break down those misconceptions.

Misconception #1: A Home is like an ATM

I observed that Americans during the housing boom often considered their home investment to be like an ATM. They eagerly "borrowed" against their magically-appearing equity without a thought for the consequences. But, like the winter weather in Texas, the beautiful highs are always followed by the miserable lows, and just when home values seemed like they would never stop climbing, they suddenly plummeted, forcing hundreds of thousands of families into financial crisis.

Treating a home as an ATM was a notorious practice during the housing boom, and it is still common for people to pull money out of their homestead to pay for large expenses such as college tuition (which I will discuss shortly). This is a thoughtless practice. Increasing the amount you owe to the bank—for any reason—only prolongs the duration of repaying your mortgage. Ultimately, this thwarts your ability to utilize the benefits of being free of home debt. Therefore:

The first cardinal rule: Don't borrow against your home equity.

Misconception #2: (Re)financing is a good idea

Traditionally, refinancing is referred to as the practice of replacing an existing (home) debt with another (home) debt under different terms. I distinguish the term "refinancing" a little differently. My definition converts the word "refinancing" to "re-financing," or said another way, "financing again." "Re-financing" occurs in two instances: when a homeowner is refinancing an existing home and when he or she is buying another homestead.

In the traditional instance of refinancing an existing home mortgage, the purpose is usually to replace a loan that carries a higher interest rate with a loan carrying a lower interest rate, affording the home-owner a lower monthly payment.

However, what most loan officers won't tell you (they're in the business of selling mortgages after all) is that lower interest rates don't always mean that refinancing an existing home loan is the best choice. Refinancing a home loan can be a smart choice for some, but not all. People often pat themselves on the back for negotiating a better interest rate than their neighbor when they refinance, but what they don't realize is that they just extended the life of their mortgage back to another thirty-year note!

We also "re-finance" when we buy another homestead. Every time we upsize, downsize or buy another homestead, for whatever reason, and acquire a mortgage to do so, we are "financing again." In other words, we are re-financing ourselves into another thirty-year commitment.

I own a real estate company. I make money every time a homeowner decides it's time to make a move and buy a home. I stand to lose by telling you this, but you should stop trying to keep up with the Joneses. We live in a society that believes advancement to a higher income also means advancing to a higher mortgage payment; in other words, we view a sizable promotion as a ticket into a larger, better home.

Starting in early 2014, lenders loan up to a 43% debt-to-income ratio. I recommend that your entire ARMe not exceed 45% if you want enough income to save and invest appropriately. Now, do you have any wonder why most Americans don't—or rather can't—save and invest? Also, remember: your home equity is not an ATM. A more expensive home in a better part of town does not mean more to borrow against later on.

In fact, it means the opposite. Do the math. In most cases, every time we refinance we acquire another thirty-year note. If, at every opportunity, we refinance for the sake of lowering the interest rate of our current home mortgage or refinance in terms of purchasing a new home, at what age will we be debt free? I do not mean to only buy once and never buy again. I'm simply saying that before choosing to refinance, make sure your mortgage debt is part of your overall financial consideration. Thus, I introduce you to the second cardinal rule:

The second cardinal rule: Don't "refinance" your homestead without first having a financial strategy in place.

For example, Garry and I sold our more modest home in another part of town to buy into the school district we wanted for our children. This decision doubled the size of our mortgage and increased the amount we paid in property taxes, but we considered this to be the best choice for our family and therefore took on the additional debt. We took on a thirty-year note to afford the payments at the time of purchase, which meant we wouldn't pay off our note until reaching our early/mid-sixties. However, we did set up our account with bi-monthly payments and made an additional principal payment each year, bringing down the length of our note by several years.

Five years into that mortgage, interest rates suddenly dropped. We took advantage of that opportunity to convert our thirty-year note to a fifteen-year, enabling us to automatically shave ten years off our mortgage expense, while spending roughly the same towards our mortgage each month. But, better yet, by employing the same bi-monthly and additional principal payments, we will be mortgage-debt free in less than a decade!

Car Loans

In our country, car loans are a way of life: we plan to always have one. Following the same logic we use to justify getting a home refinanced, most of us don't keep the car we've paid off . Instead, the norm is to either lease a car to get a fancier car we can't afford, or to trade-in for the nicer/newer model when the last loan is paid. This thereby continues our car loan expense.

The average car payment in the U. S. is reported to be $475. If that car buyer were to invest that $475 for twenty years instead of continuing to roll it into the next car, at a 9% interest rate, he or she would be worth over $320,000. Just consider what you could do with that kind of money.

That brings me to my third cardinal rule:

The third cardinal rule: Don't lease a car, and if at all possible, don't carry a car loan.

If you do need to borrow to buy a car in order to have a safe, reliable means of transportation, then I suggest you follow the practice of pay-ing off your car note in as few months as possible. In other words, opt for the thirty-six-month rather than the sixty-month loan. Not only are you extending your debt-payoff with the sixty month by an additional three years, you'll pay twice as much in interest for the same car. Going for the lower number may mean a less expensive car than the one you want, but remember, if you have to stretch out your payments so you can "afford it," that's a clue that you can't afford it. In fact, if you have to finance a car for sixty months, you shouldn't be buying a car—or at least not that particular car.

Also, once you make a car purchase, make sure to get the most value from it, driving that car until it doesn't drive any longer. With proper maintenance, vehicles today will last more than 100,000 miles, en-abling you time to save for the outright purchase of your next car. Resist the consumerist urge, and buy a new vehicle only when the first one meets the end of its life. And by all means, never have more than one car loan.

Credit Card Balances

According to many studies, the average indebted American house-hold credit card balance for 2013 was over $15,000, with an average interest rate of 16%. In addition, an astounding 60% of credit card users don't pay off their balances each month. Credit cards tend to carry the highest interest rates of all borrowed money. Worse, they usually charge compound interest as the fee for borrowing the mon-ey, as opposed to the simple interest charged on others types of loans.

When it comes to debt, it's important to understand the difference between simple interest and compound interest. Basically, simple interest is interest paid on the original principal only. Compound interest is the interest paid not only on the original principal, but also on all accrued interest. Unpaid balances compound quickly when the interest owed compounds daily, which is why many people find it im-possible to get out of credit card debt even after they quit additional spending. Remember, you want to *earn* compound interest, not pay it.

There is a maxim that says, "the borrower is servant to the lender." Nothing is more true when it comes to credit card debt; keeping a balance on your cards keeps big banks in the business of owning you. My maxim: Be the lender and not the borrower, so that you can do what you want.

The huge amount of American credit card debt is the most apparent indication that we are accustomed to "borrowing" a life we can't afford, but credit cards themselves are not the problem. Use of credit cards can actually make a lot of financial sense. For example, Garry and I put as many of our household expenses as possible on our credit cards to accumulate points and other incentives. In fact, most of our travel expenses are paid for via points accumulated from our credit card purchases. However, we make sure to always carry a zero balance by reconciling all of the charges and paying off the cards in full each month.

The fourth cardinal rule: Don't borrow a life you can't afford.

College Loans

Student loans (borrowed by both the student and his or her parents) comprise one of the four largest categories of debt. As I mentioned earlier, the amount owed on student loans in this country is staggering. This is yet another example of living a life we can't afford, because living within our means would incorporate saving and/or investing for a child's education, assuming we intend for him or her to go to college.

Because it is so easy to borrow in a country where people have little education or knowledge about the cost of borrowing, we have an American epidemic on our hands. Parents have borrowed—many against home equity—to the point that they forestall or even eliminate their ability to comfortably retire. Students have borrowed so much that a good portion of them will be shackled to debt repayment for decades to come, shattering many of their financial hopes and life dreams.

The fifth cardinal rule: Don't just live in the financial present, but also plan your financial future.

What if you have a college-age student, but lack savings to pay for his or her tuition? Many people today believe that a degree is the only ticket to a financially-stable future, but I'm not so sure. In my son's junior year of high school, I actually counseled him to spend time in Europe after high school graduation in lieu of following the traditional college track that would be taken by his closest friends. He asked me, "Mom, if going straight into college from high school is such a bad idea, why is everyone doing it?" My reply: "The reason to question that path is precisely because everyone is taking it."

Again, I have an iconoclastic nature, as you can probably tell by now: I question the norm. And in this case, I believe the ROI (return on investment) of a European "education" will be much greater than the ROI on the first year of a traditional college education for my son. So far, I think I've been proven right. Not only did my son's trip cost us much less than a semester at college, but he also, in just the first six months of travel, learned life skills such as independence, negotiating, decision-making, and gratitude. He even learned how to "budget." He quickly realized that running out of money has harsh consequences—in his case, sleeping on a cold, wet park bench in a foreign place and subsisting on bread and water until his next monthly installment. I'm not sure if my son will choose to attend college after completing his world travels, but I know that my daughter, who will graduate high school in 2014, is intent on it. I believe both avenues have a lot of value to offer my children.

I'm sharing this story so you realize that, even if you are not financially prepared to send your child to college, you have options. Student loans should be a last resort, taken on only after a careful discussion with your children about their future path, and after they apply for as many scholarships and grants as possible. Listen to your instincts: don't force your children into higher education simply because everyone else is doing it, especially when it will put you deeper into the red. I suggest talking to your financial planner about your particular situation.

How are you feeling? Do you think some of your old mindset around debt has been punctured, allowing new ways of thinking to emerge? I hope that, at this point, you've come to understand the long-term damage that debt can bring, perhaps even obstructing your intention to live a goodLife. If so, then you're ready to discuss methodology for paying off unwanted debt.

If you carry a lot of debt, your question may be: "Where do I start?" As with everything, there are many recommended systems for debt payoff. Personally, I like Dave Ramsey's "Debt Snowball" technique. He suggests these steps:

1. List your debts in order, with the smallest payoff or balance first (not the highest interest rate).
2. Next, in terms of order, list those with the highest interest rates.
3. As you pay off credit cards, use the aggregate of these old payments towards paying off the next card on the list [see figure 8].

DEBT reduction (Dr)

Credit Card #1	$ -
Minimum Monthly Payment	
Additional Payment	
Total Credit Card #1	$ -
Credit Card #2 Minimum Monthly Payment	$ -
Credit Card #3 Minimum Monthly Payment	$ -
Extra House Payment	$ -
Extra Auto Loan Payment	$ -
TOTAL DEBT reduction (Dr)	$ -

[figure 8]

This process is an excellent standard that can be molded to basically any debt payoff objective. For example, I mentioned earlier that the only outstanding personal debt Garry and I have is mortgage debt on our homestead and investment properties. To address the payoff of these loans, we elaborated on the Debt Snowball formula. Here's our five-step formula:

1. We create a spreadsheet of all of our loans (debts), organized in order of lowest pay-off to highest pay-off.
2. We choose to pay the absolute minimum amount allowed on each loan.
3. We set a goal to pay off loan 1 (the loan with the lowest payoff). Choosing the lowest payoff enables us the opportunity to pay it off the quickest.
4. We "find" money in our budget that's better spent going towards debt payoff; we allocate that amount, adding it to the payment on loan 1. The additional money going towards principal increases the velocity of payoff, thereby decreasing the time required to pay off that note.
5. When loan 1 is paid off, we combine the total amount we were paying monthly on note 1 (payment amount + a little extra) and combine it to the payment of loan 2, systematically setting the additional amount to go towards principal of loan.

That system continues until all loans are paid off. One pro-tip I swear by is to automate as much as possible. As I shared before, our method for systematically paying off our home mortgage as soon as possible was to set up bi-weekly payments (every other week), thereby paying an extra mortgage payment per year. It's human nature to avoid the unpleasant; in regards to paying debt, we all find excellent reasons for missing an additional payment now and again. Automating the payments keeps you from putting all that responsibility on yourself.

As I've stated, there are many methods of debt-reduction, but I love this method. With each loan payoff there is a great feeling of success. It's part of the good feeling of watching your money grow—in this case you experience yourself becoming more in control of your financial situation each time another debt is paid off.

You'll need to choose what debt to start paying off first (talk to your financial planner if you need help), create a payoff plan, automate it, and then sit back and let the system work for you. It's not quite that easy, but then again, not much more difficult.

Exercise 3.4: Budgeting My goodLife Debt Payoff

That was a lot of information, so let's try putting some of it into practice. I can't tell you exactly what debt to unload because I'm not your financial planner, but I can advise that you start with the debt that charges you compound interest, which is usually credit card debt.

For reasons specified earlier, if you carry credit card debt you must create a strategy for paying off that debt as soon as possible. And, moving forward, keep in mind that there really is no justification for having credit card debt (expect in the case of an emergency with no other option—but that's when you should use your rainy-day fund). A credit card balance is proof that you are living a life you can't afford. Knowing what you know now, you'll undoubtedly agree that it's imperative to stop spending on credit cards and to pay them off.

For the exercise below, start your debt payoff plan by taking a stab at your credit card debt.

Tools:
- Credit card calculator
- All credit card statements/balances
- An Excel Spreadsheet

Credit Card	Lowest Balance	Minimum Payment
CC1	$ -	$ -
CC2	$ -	$ -
CC3	$ -	$ -
CC4	$ -	$ -
CC5	$ -	$ -
CC6	$ -	$ -

[figure 9] Credit Card payoff Chart

ex. 03.4

Instructions:

1. List your credit card debts in order of smallest payoff/balance to highest.

2. Enter in the table above [see figure 9] the minimum payment for each respective credit card.

3. Determine how much additional money you will pay above the minimum payment on credit card 1 each month:
    $ _____

4. Set up "additional pay" with online banking.

5. Using a credit card calculator, determine the guess-timated date that credit card 1 will be paid off (and mark on your calendar) _____
    - Do not add an additional dollar to the balance of your credit cards (or obtain new cards)
    - Follow this protocol until your debt is paid off. Make no changes and don't cheat.
    - With the payoff of each credit card, it's essential to combine the dollar amount of that payment with the aggregate amount of ALL credit card payments that came before it.

6. Calculate the combined minimum balance of all of your credit cards x 12 (or number of months left in the year):
    $ _____

7. Add #5 and #6 together: $ _____

8. Add this number to the respective debt payoff section of your budget.

ex. 03.4

Once you complete this exercise, you will have budgeted your credit card debt payoff, allowing you to soon be free of high interest debt.

Now I wish you to make another promise to yourself. Read the words below aloud, realizing what they mean for your habits, and write them in the space I've provided:

"I will not add any balance to my credit card!"

_____

Finally, set a goal to be 100% debt free. If you didn't include this goal in your dreamLife before, do it now. A goodLife is a debt-free life.

Recap: If you completed this exercise, you now have a plan to pay down and pay off your credit cards. Did you make a promise to yourself to not add anything more to your credit cards? Not a single expense. Remember, if you are purchasing items on your credit card, you are living a life you can't afford, and it will hurt you in the future. Commit to living a life you can afford. Also, did you add the debt-free goal to your goal sheet? If not, I highly recommend it. It's imperative to living a goodLife in the present and future.

ex. 03.4

Part 4 | Budgeting My goodLife's Little Luxuries

> "The art is not in making money, but in keeping it."
>
> *Proverb*

When it comes to the financial side of living a goodLife, a couple of different schools of thought exist. Some believe one should sacrifice all of life's little luxuries today until all savings and investments are on track and they're completely debt-free. At the other extreme are those who believe they can do anything they want to do (or buy anything they want to buy) today and the future will just work itself out.

I sit somewhere in the middle. My belief and practice is to enjoy my goodLife today *and* tomorrow. I don't want to live completely without today or completely without tomorrow. I thus find myself continuously traversing a delicate balance between living a life of luxury today and creating an opportunity to live an equally good life of luxury in retirement. I don't think it's necessary to sacrifice one life for the other, but I do think we have to plan and act on behalf of both.

For this reason, I never advocate entirely eliminating all of life's little luxury expenses from your budget, even in a personal situation that includes little savings and a lot of debt. I believe that luxury purchases, if planned for, can be part of life's celebration. There is a caveat, however. Those intent on building wealth—which we've ascertained is a must if we wish to live a goodLife during retirement age—must think and act inside three philosophical notions, all of which are extremely unpopular:

1. We are not entitled to anything in life. We are not entitled to the fairytale house with the white picket fence, nor the fancy car needed to impress our friends, nor the latest model big screen TV for our Sunday football enjoyment, nor even health-care (paid for by others).

2. We always have a choice, and each choice has a consequence. Some consequences may be positive while others are negative; some will be experienced in the short-term and others in the long-term. Because we live in a universe of cause and effect, every choice (cause) we've made in our lives up to this exact point in time has put us exactly where we are at this exact point in time (effect). If we're happy with our lives, we have been the cause of it through our choices. If we are dissatisfied with our lives, we have been the cause of it through our choices. It took me well into my thirties to finally realize that every single time in my life when things were totally 'effed up,' I was there! I was always the common denominator, even though other people, places, and things may have been different. Once I noticed this, I realized that I could never again point my finger to anyone but myself as someone to blame. That wasn't easy; it certainly felt better to point my finger in a different direction than at myself, but after this epiphany I was finally able to take control of my life and my happiness.

3. We don't already know everything. For example, I think we all know those certain annoying someones who just cannot be wrong. They won't ever admit failure. They think they know everything and want everyone else to exalt their smartness. Without fail they negatively judge those who think and act differently than they do. A clear picture of a specific person probably comes to mind for all of us, right? However, I doubt that the person who comes to mind is ourselves—even if we know

we are capable of sometimes acting this way. To build wealth, we must rid ourselves of this dangerous self-delusion. Arrogance prevents us from taking advantage of important growing opportunities.

In fact, my own arrogance caused me to almost miss out on one of my life's most influential learning experiences. Not long ago, I sat in on a talk by David Bach, the best-selling author of many books written about one of my favorite topics of conversation: money. I was star struck and thrilled to be in the front row admiring him as he shared his secrets live, on the big stage. However, I'm ashamed to say that I didn't expect to learn much. I arrogantly assumed I had already heard of and applied everything he would be talking about to my own money management, thinking, and practices.

I was wrong. Within the first thirty minutes, as he explained his famous "Latte Factor," Bach knocked the arrogance (and breath) right out of me.

If you had been sitting next to me as Bach told his story, you might have noticed my body spontaneously shiver or see goose bumps appear on my arms. I had experienced what I call an "Aha!" moment, a shift that changed my entire perspective on life. I realized in that instant that, even though I had read about the Latte Factor, I really didn't understand the lesson behind it. Perhaps it was the way Bach spoke, but I actually thought to myself, "Damn, I've had it all wrong." I had entered that brightly lit room feeling like one of those terrible know-it-alls, but I was paradoxically happy to realize my lack of knowledge.

If I had not let go of my arrogant mindset, I would have missed my precious Aha! moment, and you would not be reading this book. Let me explain. The Latte Factor, a term coined and trademarked by Bach, is based on the idea that, to live a goodLife, we must look at the small things we spend our money on every day. The example Bach uses is daily Starbucks lattes. The Latte Factor is based on a true story, but also functions as a metaphor for how we waste small amounts of money on small things. It is meant to help people acknowledge how they irresponsibly spend money.

Over the years, I have heard more people than I can count say, "I don't have enough money to save." The fact is, that's probably not true for most people. If, for an entire week, we were to record daily all items we buy—just as people seriously trying to lose weight record every calorie—I think Bach's approach would prove that most of us have more than enough money to start saving. In fact, outside of this course, I challenge you to do the following exercise: for a full week, record your daily "miscellaneous" spending, arriving at a seven-day total. I suggest you download Bach's calculator to make this exercise really easy: http://www.finishrich.com/lattefactor/.

But, for now, take a guess:

1. How much do you think you spend each week on those metaphorical lattes? $_____

2. Multiply that number by 52 (weeks): $_____

3. How much would that amount be worth in ten years if invested at a 10% return? $_____

That's some serious money! Before the conference, I indulged in a Starbucks Grande Americano every day—at a cost of $3.50, not to mention the valuable time spent waiting in line. After I completed the exercise above for myself, I realized I was spending $1,260 a year on coffee that I could easily make at home for a fraction of the cost. More important, my $1,260, if invested instead of spent, would in ten years grow to over $20,000!

But that isn't even the best part. The shock came when I realized that the $1,260 a year on my coffee wasn't the total I was spending on my life's little luxuries. In reality, I was easily spending $100 per week. Using a simple compounding calculator, that $100 weekly spending habit was costing me $327,613 that I could have earned in twenty years if I had invested it with a 10% return. And that's just *my* spending. Garry probably spends a little more than that each week, so if our combined $250 weekly spending was invested at 10%, the money we could save would earn us $819,032. Now, that's real money!

My Aha! moment was the realization that I was living a life I couldn't afford because my definition of "luxury" was all wrong. I considered luxuries to be those high-end consumables I drooled over in the Robb Report. Promising myself to never become a high-income poor person again, I had always patted myself on the back for being able to abstain from desirable luxury purchases such as the Rolex watch or the amazing shoes at Neiman Marcus. I was even proud of my ability to walk through Nordstrom's without opening my wallet. What I didn't realize was that I was still living a life of luxury—only now, instead of large expenses, I had filled my life with little luxuries.

What is your definition of luxury?

Today, I consider a luxury to be anything and everything I spend on consumption that isn't part of my ARMe and spent before I've adequately saved and invested. "But why?" you ask. The simple answer is because until we have enough of our monthly income going towards the savings and investments necessary to support our life now and when we're re-tired, the hard cold reality is that we can't (really) afford the extras.

For my planning, I think of two categories of luxuries. There are the little luxuries such as Starbucks drinks, restaurant and bar tabs, cable bills, retail store purchases, and manicures and pedicures. And, the larger luxury expenses such as a new car, boat or home improvement. The first category is part of my monthly spending and the second is what I save for and purchase at a later date in cash.

Thinking of "luxuries" this way is powerful because it allows you to properly plan for your desired little luxury expenses so as not to cut them out completely, but keep them in their proper order of spending. Keep in mind that you may need to cut out a portion of the little luxuries from your budget to free up money that can be reallocated to savings and investment or debt payoff [see figure 10].

If you are anything like me, the idea of cutting luxury items is a big pill to swallow. I didn't like the idea of giving up my cherished Americano. But I liked even less the idea of sacrificing $800,000 that could support my lifestyle when I am sixty. In America's culture of immediate gratification, it's dificult to accept the need to save and invest in order to live a long goodLife.

If we feel entitled to our life's little luxuries, and therefore refuse to give them up at the expense of saving and investing, our choices are guaranteed to eventually catch up with us. I compare this to the chain smoker who knows the health risks associated with the habit, but chooses to continue. Such a choice postpones the pain and suffering of withdrawal, but will ultimately have a dire result. Living a life we can't afford is usually the result of a similar intoxicating addiction. It is guaranteed to produce a different kind of pain and suffering, but pain and suffering all the same.

little luxuries (ll)
Household Updates
Housekeeper
Yard Maintenance
Pool Maintenance
Department Store Purchases
Shoes
Non-Essential Clothing
Mani | Pedi
Massage
Gifts Given
Restaurants
Happy Hour
Entertainment
Cable TV
Spotify
Non-Essential Household Items
TOTAL little luxuries (ll) $ -

[figure 10] Little Luxuries Chart of Accounts

As I said earlier, little luxuries in my opinion are okay—if, and only if:

1. You don't feel entitled to them;
2. You choose them knowing the compromise you are making (luxury over saving or debt-repayment); and
3. You plan for them in your budget.

With this said, keep in mind one final cardinal rule:

The sixth cardinal rule: Only after saving and investing can we truly afford a life of luxury.

Once you've budgeted your little luxuries, you will have completed your forecasted expense budget for the year. I call the byproduct of creating your forecasted expenses in your budget your goodLife Spending Map™. It should account for all your actual spending compared to what you predicted you would spend month by month. Your goodLife Spending Map will become the guide for what you are "allowing" yourself to spend each month. Just like the concept of giving your kids an allowance, you are giving yourself an allowance (in fact, part of your monthly allowance should be your kids' allowance). If followed, your goodLife Spending Map will make sure your spending stays on track for the rest of the year, as a necessary part of building your wealth.

Here's the sequence of spending to help you remember prioritization:

Exercise 3.5: Budgeting My goodLife Little Luxuries

Now that you have your ARMe around your expenses (ha!), it's time to earmark the income you wish to spend on your little luxuries. It's likely that you are spending too much on such purchases already and, as a result, need to cut down to boost your savings and/or pay down debt. Again, I'm not suggesting that you cut out little luxuries entirely. However, I do urge you to consider which little luxuries you can do without and plan for those you can't do without in this part of your budget.

When working on this exercise, remember that little luxuries are not only large fancy purchases, but also such things as Starbucks, restaurant and bar tabs, cable bills, retail store purchases, and manicures and pedicures. Basically, any expense outside your ARMe + Savings/Investments + Debt Reduction should be considered a luxury.

Once you've completed this exercise, you will possess a very valuable tool for building your financial future. You will use this goodLife Spending Map to guide your spending for the rest of the year.

Determining and calculating your little luxuries is pretty straightforward, but does require some thinking and assessing. For example, most restaurant bills will belong in the luxury category, but a "date night" with your spouse every week could be considered an ARMe expense; after all, taking care of your marriage is critical to happiness (and wealth building). Also, some might think of a monthly massage as luxury, while others would consider it a required expense. I consider a massage to be both. I count one massage per month as a required "self-care" expense, but the remaining three a month (one per week) as a luxury.

ex. 03.5

To help complete your exercise, first find the answers to thes questions:

1. How much is your ARMe (planned + unplanned)?

   $_____

2. How much do you commit to save and invest this year?

   $_____

3. How much will you allocate towards debt payoff this year?

   $_____

4. What is the sum of these three numbers?

   $_____

5. How much did you spend last year on little luxuries (everything not included in the previous numbers)?

   $_____

Tools needed:
- Calculator
- Purple Highlighter
- All of your actual Expenditures this year
- A copy off all non-ARMe expenses—these should be highlighted in Red from a previous exercise.

Instructions:
1. Open your budget.
2. Move your actual little luxury expenses into the respective cells on your budget.

   NOTE: you should have these highlighted in red.
3. Go back over all expenses on your budget. Relocate any expenditures you now consider luxury from the ARMe, placing them in the luxury categories.

ex. 03.5

4. Highlight any "business" expenses in purple.

   For example, highlight a business happy hour taken with a prospective client. These should be moved to a business budget.

5. Add any little luxuries that you didn't indulge in last year but wish to treat yourself to this year.

6. Remove any of last year's little luxuries that you now deem unaffordable.

7. Make one more pass through, ensuring that everything appears to be in its appropriate location on your spreadsheet.

Recap:

You now have your goodLife Spending Map. How do you feel? Are you proud of the work that got you here? Has my definition of "luxury" changed any perspective for you? Will it change future actions?

ex. 03.5

Part 5 | Budgeting My Income for Allocation

> "The inability to delay gratification is the
> primary predictor of economic failure in
> life."
>
> *Brian Tracy*

The first four parts of creating a budget required that you focus on expenses, leaving you in possession of your goodLife Spending Map. Using this map as a guide to manage expenses offers you a better chance for staying on track to manifest your goodLife.

We've only focused on expenses so far, but to complete your budget we must now consider our income. The fifth part of creating your budget brings your income into the conversation. Your income is what distinguishes your complete budget (goodLife Money Map) from just your Spending Map.

Thus far, your budget creation has only taken into consideration last year's expenses as a means to create this year's budget. If your goal is for this year to look about the same as last year, financially speaking, then the budget created so far will work brilliantly as a tool for the remainder of your year.

However, if you'd like to plan this year to be different from previous years, you will want to bring your income into the equation to do so. Let's look at your spending goals and expense forecasts in terms of a percentage of income you project to earn this year.

As a guide, I'm going to share my goodLife Income Allocation Formula™ with you. The chart below [see figure 11] shows how Garry and I allocate our income to cover each category of expense. Before doing so, I must voice another disclaimer: this is meant as a reference tool only. However, this model is the only one we've found that will allow Garry and me to stay on track to earning, saving and investing enough money to live a goodLife today and a goodLife during our retirement. The percentages used are actual percentages Garry and I use to allocate our income towards the different categories of expenses.

Expense Category	Percentage of Income	Dollar Amount per $100,000 of Income
ARMe	40%	$40,000
Taxes (after deductions)	33%	$33,000
Savings	5%	$5,000
Investments	17%	$17,000
Luxuries	5%	$5,000

[figure 11] goodLife Allocation Chart™

Keep in mind that we use these allocations to forecast our spending for the year ahead. The actual numbers always deviate somewhat from what we predicted (such is life), but over the years they've averaged out as shown above.

Does anything jump out when looking at this table? I want you to notice three things in particular.

First, our total ARMe (required/necessary expenses) is 40%. This is low when you consider the fact that lenders today will loan up to 43% for a home mortgage alone, yet we allocate only 40% of our income to be used towards operating our household. This includes the cost of not only the mortgage, but also the cost of our utilities, car expenses, groceries, healthcare and self-care, and child obligations.

Being in the real estate business, I've noticed over the years that the majority of our customers choose to "borrow" the maximum amount the lender will loan them in order to purchase the "most" home the lender tells them they can afford. Because the bank says they can afford it, it must be true, right? Do your own calculation. What percentage of your income is your total ARMe? Remember that this number has to come first, and that the more you must allocate towards that expense, the less of your income will be available for investments and luxuries.

Second, taxes constitute a huge chunk of our hard-earned income —over a third. The subject of taxes can easily turn into a political conversation, which I wish to avoid here, but their effect on our budgets cannot be ignored. In my experience, people don't realize how much they pay in taxes because they are used to living on what's left of their paycheck. However, by budgeting our taxes, we are forced to consider the amount we pay, and how that chunk taken by Uncle Sam impacts our life and livelihood. This is real money that we need to consider just as necessary as any other expense on our ARMe. To grow your wealth, you must understand and account for taxes in planning your goodLife. In a larger, more philosophical sense, I urge you also to think about what taxes do to the goodLife budgets of others. Please don't wish to impose something upon others and their families that you don't wish to impose upon yourself and your family when it comes to anything in life, including taxes.

Third, the amount we allocate toward our luxury spending is only 5%. After we account for the amount required to operate our household, pay Uncle Sam, save for emergencies, and invest an adequate amount necessary to stay on our wealth-building track, there is only a small amount left over to assign to the unnecessary but desired expenses such as Starbucks, cable TV, dinners at trendy restaurants, and my mani-pedis. Granted, once all of our savings accounts are maxed out, we are allotted a little more towards luxury, but only until the need to dip into those savings and therefore the need to reallocate the amount need to replenish the account. Everything else remains pretty constant.

Now that you know the model, take a moment to consider your own income allocation. Answer the following questions to the best of your ability. Guessing at this point is okay, but try to be as accurate as possible.

1. How much income do you project to earn this year?
   $_____

2. What percentage of this income do you plan to allocate towards each of the four budget expense categories?
   - ARMe Expenses: %_____
   - Savings & Investing: %_____
   - Debt-Payoff: %_____
   - Life's Little Luxuries: %_____

The final amounts you calculate here will leave you concluding one of two things:

1. I earn enough income to be able to afford a goodLife according to the goodLife financial principles described thus far; or,

2. Even after reducing my expenses, I do not earn enough income to be able to afford the goodLife I desire, especially after taking into account the goodLife principals so far. This means I need to reduce my spending more and/or earn more income.

If you have an adequate income with which to live your goodLife—congratulations! If you realized that your income is inadequate, don't worry. Try the following exercise to make sure that you know exactly how much income is enough, and then read on to Chapter 4. I will be puncturing some traditional thoughts about income and hopefully help you come up with a plan of action.

Exercise 3.6:
Budgeting My Income for Income Allocation

It's time to complete your budget for the year. In this exercise, you will look at budgeting your expenses from an "Income Allocation" perspective as described above. If you complete and truly budget according to the numbers reflected in this exercise, you'll be well on your way to financial freedom.

To complete this exercise, make sure that you have your previously completed budget and spending map available. Completing this exercise will allow you to modify your current budget and spending map into an awesomely powerful tool for designing and planning your finances life category. Thinking and designing from this perspective is the difference between dreaming a goodLife and living one now and in the future.

Instructions:
1. Estimate your projected income for this year: $_____

2. Fill out this allocation chart to reflect your current budget

Expense Category	Current Dollar Amount Reflected in Your Budget	Percentage of Your Current Income
ARMe	$ -	ARMe $/Income
Taxes	$ -	Taxes $/Income
Savings	$ -	Savings $/Income
Investments	$ -	Investment $/Income
Luxuries	$ -	Luxuries $/Income
TOTAL	$ Total Budget Expenses	100% (if the sum is less than or greater than 100%, your calculations are off)

[figure 12] Budget Allocation Chart

ex. 03.6

3. Create a goodLife Allocation Plan™
   - My projected annual income: $_____
   - Calculate my goodLife allocation dollar amounts: Multiply my annual income by the percentages in column two and enter in column three.
   - Calculate the difference between the amount of income I would allocate using goodLife percentages versus my historical spending allocations.
   - Consider what actions are required to live my life according to a goodLife financial methodology
     - Downsize my home/rent?
     - Reduce the amount of my luxury spending?
     - Vie to pay lower taxes?
   - Revise my annual budget numbers from earlier:
   - If you wish to use an allocation approach versus a historical spending approach for establishing your budget numbers, make the necessary adjustments based on the chart below.

Expense Category	goodLife Allocation Percentage	goodLife Allocation $ amounts	Your allocation	The Difference between your allocation & the goodLife allocation
ARMe	40%	$ Column 2 x income	$ -	$ -
Taxes	33%	$ Column 2 x income	$ -	$ -
Savings	5%	$ Column 2 x income	$ -	$ -
Investment	17%	$ Column 2 x income	$ -	$ -
Luxuries	5%	$ Column 2 x income	$ -	$ -
Totals:	100%		$ -	$ -

[figure 13] goodLife Allocation Chart

ex. 03.6

What would your budget numbers be for each category if you used goodLife percentages?

What amount would you increase or reduce in order to hit the goodLife numbers?

Recap:
What did you notice as a result of completing this exercise? How does it feel? Are you willing to take the actions necessary to live a life you can afford? Can you now see why our American culture doesn't like taking on the responsibility of living a life they/we can afford?

THOUGHTS & NOTES

ex. 03.6

THOUGHTS & NOTES

ex. 03.6

Chapter IV

Step 4: Generating My goodLife Income

> "The key factor that will determine
> your financial future is not the economy;
> the key factor is your philosophy."
>
> Jim Rohn

We are done with budgeting. It's now time, in Step 4 of our goodLife Money Map, to delve into a conversation about income.

Traditional goal-setting and budgeting conversations often start with the word "income." I, however, think that the traditional sequence is out of order. That's why the income conversation is Step 4 rather than Step 1 of my Money Mapping System.

It's a natural mistake to start with income, and when we do we usually say something like this: "I want to make $50,000 more this year," or "I want to grow business revenue by 20%."

Have you ever said something similar? I find that, many times, these amounts do not logically follow any previous situation or reality. We simply know we need and want "more," so we make up a number that sounds good and attempt to commit to it. We put that "more" figure out in the universe with great excitement at the year's start, only to find ourselves falling short come December.

If you wish to increase your income but find yourself falling into the "more trap," it's likely that you won't earn a higher income this year compared to last. To avoid this pitfall, as well as to provide a better chance to increase earnings, you must know how much money is enough this year to live the lifestyle you want to be able to afford. Only by knowing how much is enough can you articulate a target income grounded in reality. This number is derived from a thoughtful and methodical practice, which inspires with a different level of importance to you. You will therefore have a stronger passion and commitment to produce this amount of income than you would have with your "more" figure.

The method I use to determine how much is enough is derived through the five-part budgeting practice I've shared with you. The cost of our lifestyle, which includes the amount we need to save, invest and reduce debt by, is our income goal. This amount, by the way, should be higher than your current earnings because it represents the cost of your desired life. I call this number the goodLife Number™.

Moving forward, your goodLife Number represents three things:

1. *The cost of living your goodLife this year.*
    Your goodLife number is the amount of money it will take to pay for your desired lifestyle this year. Remember, your ARMe represents the amount of money it will take to pay for your required life this year. Your S&I number (savings and investing) and debt payoff numbers represent the amount it will take to ensure the ability to pay for your future goodLife. Your goodLife Number will combine these amounts and also give you room for more little luxuries.

2. *The amount of money you will have to make this year.*
    Your goodLife number represents how much money you must earn to fund your lifestyle for the year. The simple fact of knowing this number, believe it or not, can ease loads of financial pressure. Your goodLife number enables you to know how much money is enough for the year to come. In other words, the elusive word "more" no longer has to be the answer.

3. *The number used to set your business/career goals.*
    Your goodLife Number is the basis of your goodBusiness goals. When you know the amount of money you must earn this year to fund your desired lifestyle, you can easily translate that number into definable, measurable goals. If attained, those goals will enable you to earn the necessary amount.

Every year since my twenties I've earned an income greater than that of the average American family. In most years, far greater. But, as I learned early on, it's not making it that matters, but keeping it. After going broke in my thirties due to irresponsible money habits,

I was committed to unlearn the thinking that got me to that undesirable place and to study the money philosophy, principles, and practices of self-made multimillionaires.

During my quest I came across an important discovery: I didn't have a philosophy about money. Let me rephrase that. I had a philosophy, but unbeknownst to me, it was a counter-productive one. This meant that, despite my hard work and best intentions, I was doomed. My unconscious made-up answer to solving all of life's problems, stemming both from my childhood experience and the culture I embraced, was "earn a high-income." Beginning. The end.

As I uncovered fundamental philosophies of the wealthy, I realized that their powerful principles were completely missing from my repertoire of understanding. Now, after years of study, I believe my most fundamental philosophy of money is well-founded.

Let me ask: what is your philosophy about money? What is your relationship to money? Do you, as I did, hold your parents' beliefs about money? Or that of your peers? Deep down, do you feel that having a lot of money is bad? Does the subject of money make you uncomfortable for some unidentifiable reason? Are you good at making money but terrible at keeping it? Or are you great at keeping it, but can't figure out how to make more of it? What is your definition of money? And, what does it mean to you?

Answering this type of question will help you discover your core beliefs about one of the most important subjects affecting your quality of life. I've shared with you my way of thinking and being so far. Now I'd like to sum up all that I've learned about money into one bite-sized piece of knowledge:

Our largest wealth-building asset is our income.

No matter how much money you make, if you tie up your income by living a life you can't afford—according to the philosophical principles

I've shared—in the end, you will lose. It may not feel like it now, but the universal principles of money are guaranteed to hold true. It's just a matter of time.

Remember that your income funds your lifestyle. If you realized at the end of the conversation on budgeting that you're living a life you can't afford—but didn't see many expenses, if any, that could be eliminated to pay off your debt, save and invest—then the only option left is to increase your income.

But how to earn more income? Obviously, just knowing our good-Life Number doesn't mean our income will automatically increase to match the established figure. It is a vital step, but ultimately we have to create a plan for increasing our income to the amount of our goodLife Number™. The first action of this plan is to rid ourselves of two other flawed definitions for the words "earning" and "income."

The word "earnings," one of the most commonly-used words associated with income, does not signify an active producer of, but rather a passive recipient of: when you earn something, you receive it from someone else. The problem with using this word is that it suggests inherent limits to your income, removing your autonomy and placing your financial fate entirely in someone else's hands.

If you recall, my philosophy is that we are ultimately responsible for our choices, so this idea of "earning" an income is not an option I'm willing to accept for myself or for you. I believe that increasing your income by more than just increments requires your active participation in the process. Therefore, I choose to use the phrase "generate an income" versus "earn an income." Can you see how that moves your income opportunity from the hands of another into your own?

Similarly, the general inclination is to define "income" as how much we are paid for the job we do. When we think of our income as numbers in someone else's checkbook, it may be intimidating to think we can demand a change. Focusing on the monetary amount neglects the real depth from where our "income" comes, and it creates us to be—again—passive recipients. Instead, consider that your income is based on your perceived value.

Therefore, the way we can increase our income is by producing more value and becoming more valuable to the others who influence our income in business. The amount we earn equals the value that another person places on the results of our job/work/offer. In other words, our value is dependent on another's perception of how valuable we are to them. This means that what we think we are worth is irrelevant. It's what others think we are worth that matters. We are not entitled to a higher income because of want, need or even tenure.

I think Jim Rohn says it best: "You don't get paid for the hour, you get paid for the value you bring to the hour." Asking yourself the following three questions will help you discover how to increase your value:

1. How can I increase the importance of my role to my employer? Or, how can I increase the importance of my product/service to my customer?
2. How can I become more beneficial, helpful, and useful to my boss? How can my product/service be more beneÿcial and necessary to the customer?
3. How can my production positively impact the bottom-line of the business unit and/or business? How can my product/service produce a bigger return for my customer?

I realize that this isn't a popular notion about the value of our individual work and income, but I believe it's true. If this idea was more widely accepted, people might realize that they have a lot more control over their incomes and livelihood than they thought. But, on the flip side, it means that we are responsible for our own incomes and livelihoods.

With this said, there are many times the value of our work is worth more in the marketplace than we currently earn, such as when another employer/customer is willing to pay more. If we find ourselves in this situation, it's still our responsibility to increase our income. It's not in the best interest of an employer or customer to pay more if they don't have to. Therefore, they will try to pay as little as possible.

As this is the reality of life (and business), it's important to gain the skill of confident negotiation. For example, if you wait for the raise you deserve, you may be waiting a long time. You must make the case that you are worth more than your current salary and negotiate high-er compensation. If you are worth it, it's likely you will get it. But be careful: if you have not proven your value, you may end up seeking another job or customer.

If you have discovered that living an affordable goodLife requires an increase in your income, rest assured that you are not alone. Based on national averages, it's clear that most Americans are in that exact situation, either because they spend too much or they do not earn enough (or a combination of both).

Whether you are an employee or an employer, increasing your income requires asking three questions:

1. Where am I today?
2. Where do I wish to be instead?
3. How am I going to get there?

Answering those questions requires these five actions:

1. Determine your Designed Income (goodLife Number).
2. Set business and career goals that correlate to generating your desired income.
3. Establish the strategies and executables necessary to achieve your goals.
4. Attach completion timelines and milestones to the executables.
5. Measure the actual results against the set goals.

In the case of an employee, personal income is a derivative of one's value perceived by the employer. So, it stands to reason that an employee must set measurable goals that positively and consequently affect their employer. If we wish to be a highly-valued team member, we must ensure that we are never considered a payroll expense. The only way to avoid this is by demonstrating that the results of your work somehow increase revenue or reduce expenses. For example, you may increase sales by assisting the sales team or reduce expenses by creating a system that decreases the number of support calls.

In the case of a business owner, personal income is a derivative of business profit. Therefore, increasing personal income is a function of growing business profits through increased revenue and lowered expenses. There are a number of ways to increase profit, so the business goals, executables, and milestones should be set to produce whatever is the desired income and expenses. Once business goals and initiatives have been set, the business owner will set their personals goals, executables, and milestones as their part of the over-all business initiative.

Whether you're an employee or employer, and whether you do or don't have suficient income, you can count on one thing: each year brings new situations, discoveries, lessons, and knowledge. Therefore, you may find it necessary to adjust your goals and goodLife Number each year when completing this Money Map process. And that's okay! Each annual budgeting exercise helps Garry and me determine how much more income we want and need in the upcoming year. That's the number we use as our "income goal" for the year.

Once you get the hang of calculating your goodLife Number, which is the cost of living your good life for a single year, you may wish to apply this skill to calculating the cost of your dreamLife.

Remember the exercise we did in Chapter 2? Refer back to the goals you wrote down in that exercise and think critically about how much you will have to earn to ultimately achieve that lifestyle. Figuring out your dreamLife Number gives you an important sense of perspective and also removes you from living in a perpetual state of "more." We cannot realistically design our lives around a word as elusive as "more."

I recommend that everyone complete this exercise, but particularly married readers. Garry and I enjoyed the philosophically-stimulating conversations we had while doing this work together; the exercise provided an opportunity to get us on the exact same page about our money. Agreeing on "how much is enough" is necessary to live the goodLife and dreamLife we both want, and enables us to stay easily committed and disciplined to remain on course. Better yet, it is rare that we disagree over money.

Exercise 4.1: Setting My goodBusiness Goals

Your goodLife Number is your annual income goal, reflecting how much living your desired life will cost this year. It's essential that you not only remember this number, but think about it and reflect on it ever day.

In fact, I recommend that you break down your goodLife Number into a per diem amount and then set an intention each morning to generate that amount of value/income that day. This practice will help you prioritize and keep you focused on the daily activities that can directly impact your income. Otherwise, it's too easy to become distracted by the noise and busy work that easily fill each day, robbing you of yet another twenty-four hours that could have been used to create your desired future.

So, now that you know your goodLife Number, you need to create a plan for generating the income you require to fund your life.

We started this program by creating personal goals. Subsequently, we determined how much income we needed to earn to fund a lifestyle that matches those goals. We will now work in the reverse, using our intended income to determine our goodBusiness and career goals.

Instructions:

1.   What was your income last year? $_____

2.   What is your goodLife Number/Income Goal?
     $_____

3.   What goals will enable you to increase income to match your goodLife Number?
     Examples: increase personal income by $50,000; renegotiate my salary to include a bonus on sales; sell 100 units;

increase business revenue by $1,000,000; learn a new skill that is congruent with increasing my income.

4. What specific work/production can you do to directly impac your income?

    Examples: create a dashboard for the sales team and monitor and track sales and assist them to hit their targets that will help the company hit its sales target of X; make 1200 prospecting calls; attend a conference relevant to learning a new skill; hire three new sales people.

5. What dates, timelines and milestone do I need to record to make sure I stay on track with the actionable items required to fulfill my goodLife career and business goals

6. How will I measure my success? How often will I measure my goals against my actual results? Put these dates on my calendar now. Who will hold me accountable?

What is my goodLife Number? _____

Once you complete this exercise, you will have your career and business goals set for the year.

Recap:
You now have your goals, executables, milestones, and tracking mechanisms in place for the year. You have everything you need to make it your best year ever, financially, and hopefully in all six "F" categories! You've worked hard to take control over your own life. How does it feel?

ex. 04.1

THOUGHTS & NOTES

ex. 04.1

Chapter V

Step 5: Establishing goodPractices for a goodLife

"My dreams are worthless, my plans are
dust, my goals are impossible. All are
of no value unless they are followed by
action."

Og Mandino

As I mentioned early on, I am a wife, mother, business owner, and keynote speaker. I am fit, healthy, happy, and feel successful in all six life categories. Many ask how I'm able to balance all these different and equally demanding life concerns. I attribute my ability to balance to intense planning and practice.

My life is very planned. If you were to look at the week-view on my calendar, you wouldn't find too many white spaces. On any given day, you might see a schedule that looks something like this:

8:30–9:00	Set intentions and objectives for the day
9:00–9:30	Meeting on site
9:45–10:15	Write 300 words for blog
10:15–10:30	Email, return calls, and check social media
10:30–11:30	Sketch next keynote speech
11:30–12:30	Take daughter to lunch
12:30–1:00	Email and calls
1:00–1:30	Meditate
1:30–3:00	Time block for sales calls
3:00–4:30	Meeting off-site
4:30–5:30	Run with Wendy
5:30–7:30	Financial date with Garry
7:30–9:00	Massage
Before bed	Read

If you look at a future month-view, you might find days blocked for a preplanned quarterly marriage retreat or a preplanned vacation. On another month, you might see one three-day block to attend a conference on business planning, while another block is designated to deliver a keynote speech at a conference. Peppered throughout my annual calendar, you will notice, are days that end at noon with nothing scheduled for the remainder of the day. These are days, usually at the end of a sizable project that required a lot of headspace and production, where I put a stop-time to my structure; I leave the rest of the day unplanned to do whatever comes to mind at that moment. Usually it's spent meeting up with a friend for an afternoon or hanging out at the local Milk and Honey day spa for some pampering (allocated in my budget, of course).

At first glance, some might think this level of planning too calculated, rigid and constrained. Others may think I'm handcuffed to a calendar. On the contrary, this level of planning offers me the exact opposite—it gives me freedom. The planning amplifies my capacity to get every-thing accomplished that I want to accomplish. Freedom and happiness come with knowing I'm fulfilling my objectives in all six F's. This level of planning also keeps me distant from the recurrent breakdowns, chaos and genuine stress I experienced in my younger days of "flying by the seat of my pants."

The other secret to my ability to live a more balanced, relaxed, and happy life is in my discipline of converting as many things as possible into recurrent practices. Another name for recurrent practices is "habits." My ability to balance my life is largely due to my desire and ability to simplify things that tend to get complicated. So much complication in my life seems to stem from a need to think, plan, discuss, debate, and or decide something. This begs the question: "What complications can I remove from my life?"

I've never left a "high-performance" conference where some version of this equation wasn't imparted: good habits = intended results. I whole-heartedly accept this high-performer axiom as true, but I think the real power and beauty of recurrent practices and habits extends even deeper. The true essence of our habits lies in their ability to help simplify our lives. A sweet simplicity exists when we take the thinking, planning, discussing, debating, and deciding completely out of the equation. Recurrent practices and habits can do just that.

As part of my effort to simplify, I convert as many important activities and actions as possible into standard practices. That is, I turn as many important things as I can into habits. For example, Sunday is massage. Monday is family sushi-dinner night. Mondays, Wednesdays, and Fridays are running days, and Tuesday and Saturdays are weight days. Every morning from 7:00–7:30 and every afternoon from 1:00–1:30 is meditation time. For easy remembering, I have all my annual health exams scheduled during my birth month. My therapist, chiropractor and other self-care appointments are pre-scheduled for the year on the same day and time each month. I have followed these practices for years, but I always keep in mind that life is life. Therefore, I remain flexible so that I can change my schedule when necessary (it changes all the time).

As I've mentioned before, I believe that we are 100% responsible for producing our own lives—the lives we want and the lives we don't want. Our current situation is a product of all the choices we've made up until now, and no one forces us to make those choices. It's this truth that causes one person to succeed at life while another fails. Coming from privilege certainly offers a head start to some over those less advantaged, but it's no guarantee. Besides, whose success do we respect more: the person who was fed with a silver spoon or the underdog?

"Success" is yet another word possessing different meanings. Success means different things to different people, and I imagine that you have a particular definition in mind as you read this passage. I prefer to think of success in terms of fulfillment. To me, fulfillment is a feeling; I feel fulfilled just like I might feel happy or sad. Therefore, I measure my own success according to how I feel. If I am achieving my goals and feel pleased and content, I consider myself successful. For example, I consider myself successful in the area of body and health when I feel healthy and full of vitality and like the way I look. Why is it that some people become accomplished at personal fulfillment while others find themselves disappointed with parts of their lives or overall circumstances? If we conducted a survey, we'd likely get different answers from each person answering that question. A myriad of different qualities can yield success. If asked the sources of my own personal and professional success, I could give a long laundry list of principles and skills that I consider important, but they all boil down into these five categories:

1. Intention.

   Everything starts with what we intend, whether we are aware of it or not. For example, our kid may not think he or she intends to get into drugs and alcohol. However, by being intent on hanging out with friends who do, our child ensures his or her future deviant behavior. Without a declared desire, aim, goal, or plan, our intentions remain subconscious, causing us to dri˙ wherever life takes us. But set intentions are a rudder that steers us along the course of life. Successful people declare their intentions.

2. Commitment.

   A commitment is a promise to cause something. If I commit to losing ten pounds, I am saying, "I promise to cause the loss of ten pounds." Holding a commitment is the action of causing or carrying out a promise. Successful people not only make bold commitments; they also remember and fulfill them consistently.

3. Discipline.

   Discipline is a methodical, self-governed way of practice. It's a way of being, and comes from a commitment to fulfill on promises made to others and to ourselves. Nobody likes discipline because it's uncomfortable, but its power is that it stands in the way of our psychology. For example, if I have an exercise discipline, I say no to happy hour and go for a run even though I'd rather hang out with my co-workers. Successful people are disciplined enough to take required action even when they don't feel like it.

4. Practice.

We may have intention, commitment, and discipline, but practice is the actual action. Our practices are our conscious habits. Most habits are those unthinking, automatic choices that are part of everyday life—as inconsequential as taking the same route to work every day or as weighty as having the bowl of ice cream each night after dinner. To succeed, we must intentionally create powerful habits that become our best practices for fulfillment. Then we keep that practice until it no longer works for us or until we find or learn a better one.

5. Accountable.

Being accountable means being responsible. Where many people try to be as minimally responsible as possible, or push their lack of responsibility onto others, successful people take full responsibility for their lives. They don't blame others when things don't work out as intended, and they are disciplined in holding themselves accountable to their commitments. They may also have other methods of high accountability such as coaches or accountability partners.

Success in any endeavor requires these skills, but let me make an example of the objective of this book: to live a goodLife we can afford.

- First, we must start by setting an intention to live a goodLife. Setting that intention requires that we ask, "What is a goodLife to me and how much does it cost?"

- Since living a goodLife requires financial wealth, setting that intention requires that we learn the principals for earning, saving, and investing enough to live a goodLife for its entirety.
- After setting the intention, we must commit to always act in alignment with our intention, which means committing to live a life we can really afford.
- Once we make the commitment, we must acquire a discipline for holding that commitment true. We must acquire a money discipline and become disciplined when it comes to spending—or, rather, not spending. Our discipline gives us power over our minds when we need it (as, for instance, when our mind tell us that the immediate gratification from buying a big screen TV will feel so good).
- Even with the best intentions, we will fall flat if we don't develop a recurrent practice for managing money and building wealth. The best method is through the act of budgeting. We must remain disciplined to the monthly act of reconciling our expenses against our spending plan as part of our budgeting practice and financial review.
- Finally, we must accept that we are fully responsible for our lives and therefore create methods for staying accountable to our commitments, thus turning out the life we want for ourselves and those we care most deeply for.

At this point, I hope I've helped you set an intention of living a good-Life, convinced you to commit to living a life you can afford, and encouraged you to be more disciplined with your money.

Now I wish to share a standard practice that will give you a framework for setting your goodFinancial practices. I will leave it up to you to be accountable to holding everything you've learned in place.

Each Year:
- Create an annual budget and break it down into a monthly spending plan. Follow the five-step budgeting process as described.

- Set up a Household Holding Account (checking account) to which you deposit all income.
    - Total deposits at the end of the year should equal your annual income.
    - After year one, you will want to reconcile your Household Holding Account by determining how much money, if any, is in the account to start the new year.
- Set up Online Bill Pay for all recurrent bills, pulling from your Household Holding Account. Set up online bill pay for any additional bills you acquire during the year.
- Set up automatic sweeps from your Household Holding Account to other savings accounts according to what you designate as part of your income allocation derived from your budget creation.
- Sweep designated income into: tax holding account, reserves account, college account, investments (saving account and/or actual investments), vacation account, and/or luxury purchases account.
- Make sure to sweep the additional amount you've committed towards the debt of choice noted in your debt-payoff strategy.

Each Week

- Review and reconcile your finances as a weekly standard practice.

    I recommend choosing a day/time that consistently stays the same. Garry and I dedicate one hour each Saturday towards weekly reconciliation. It only requires an hour per week to stay fully on top of our finances. But if we miss a week (good excuse or bad), we pay the consequence, be-cause it always requires more than two hours the following week to make up for the one missed. This alone is enough to keep us on task.

Each Month

- Budget (verb) for the month:

- Record your actual expenses into each of the line items on your budget chart of accounts in your accounting software (this can be automated).
- Compare your actual expenses to your forecasted expenses.
- Assess the situation: How are you doing? Is your spending in alignment with your spending plan? How is your debt-payoff going? Are your savings growing? Have you reached your max savings and can therefore turn off the automatic sweep?

Each Quarter

• Budget (verb) for the quarter.
- Compare your first quarter actual income and expenses to your projected income and expenses
- Review your balance sheet and note your net worth.
- Make adjustments to next quarter's forecast that better reflect the actual trend from the past 3 months.

Remember that this exact practice starts anew with the beginning of every calendar year.

If you're married, I recommend adopting an additional goodFinancial practice that Garry and I have incorporated into our lives; it's something we cherish and look forward to. We have a monthly "date night" at our favorite restaurant to discuss money. After the monthly reconciliation practice of our budget, we review our current financial standing, which includes reviewing our personal profit and loss statement (our budget) for the past month and our personal balance sheet.

In addition, we plan a "date weekend" once per quarter. We take three days to review our annual goals, plans, budgets, and balance sheet, determining whether we are on track for the quarter based on our forecasts. It never fails that we were a little ambitious when setting our goals the previous November. Consequently, our budget and reports usually require a little adjusting, but it feels good to know exactly where we are with our household finances.

As I said earlier, I especially enjoy the review of our net worth reflected on the balance sheet. I love watching it grow, and we both enjoy talking about actions we can take to help it do so. Our most recent conversation resulted in the decision to bundle the loans of several of our investment properties at a much lower aggregate interest rate. We also decided to invest a portion of our current "investment savings" into a technology startup that we assess as having a high probability of success (and will provide a nice return if our assessment is correct).

Garry especially loves our monthly date night because seeing our money grow makes me frisky. Is there any wonder why our money talk and money practice is one of the secret ingredients to our great marriage?

Exercise 5.1: goodPractices for a goodLife

Your assignment in the last session was to set the business goals you must hit if you're to earn the income needed to fund your good-Life this year. Now, using your goodLife Allocation Chart and your goodBusiness goals, let's create a financial practice for life.

Tools:
- Your preferred accounting software
- Online checking and savings account
- Your goodLife Income Allocation
- Printer and paper

Instructions:
1. Divide each of your annual budget numbers by twelve to calculate a monthly amount.
2. Transfer your monthly budget numbers into a bona fid budget in your accounting software of choice. As I mentioned earlier, I recommend Mint for both household and solo-preneur budgets. Garry and I use QuickBooks for both household and business accounts because we have payroll accounting, business reporting, and other business accounting requirements.
3. Set up online bill pay for all recurrent bills.
4. Set up automatic sweeping from your household aggregate account into various select savings accounts. This will require setting up new savings accounts.
5. Set up automatic investment sweeps. This will require talking to your financial planner to determine what invesments you wish to automate with monthly installments.
6. Create a Financial Best Practices Checklist, storing it where it's easy to retrieve when doing monthly reconciliations.
7. Follow the checklist!

ex. 05.1

The following are my Best Practices for managing my finances: (see Appendix for Financial Best Practices Checklist):

	Liabilities	Liabilities
My ARMe:	$ -	$ -
*Planned	$ -	$ -
*Unplanned	$ -	$ -
My Savings	$ -	$ -
My Investments	$ -	$ -
My Luxuries	$ -	$ -

[figure 14] **Best Practices Chart**

Questions:

- Can I reduce my ARMe expenses?
- How much debt have I paid off?
- How much am I saving?
- How much am I investing?
- What little luxuries can I go without until I'm on track with my saving and investing?
- How can I increase my income?
- What will I invest in? Real Estate, Index funds, PreTax Retirement plan?

Monthly:

- ☐ Pay bills.
- ☐ Sweep the monthly budgeted amounts for the different savings and investing commitments into the respective accounts.
- ☐ Import actual expenses into budget.
- ☐ Reconcile all accounts.
- ☐ Assess the budget versus actual numbers, adjusting budget numbers if necessary.
- ☐ Are there any action items? For example, can I make a call to a credit card company to try and get a lower interest rate?

ex. 05.1

Quarterly:
- ☐ Review my Required ARMe expenses.
- ☐ Reduce any Required ARMe expenses.
    For example, my cell phone is an ARMe expense, but can I lower the number of minutes?
- ☐ Review the savings for Unplanned ARMe expenses.
    Do I need to replenish any withdrawn monies? If so, modify the budget accordingly.
- ☐ Review the savings and investments accounts.
    How much do I have in savings? Is it growing? What is my net worth?
- ☐ Assess investment account.
    Is it time to invest?
- ☐ Review my debt payoff schedule.
    Am I reducing my debt?

Annually:

Step 1 | Reflecting on my goodLif

Step 2 | Setting my goodLife Goals
- Part 1: Visualizing and Inventing my dreamLife
- Part 2: Setting My goodLife Goals

Step 3 | Money Mapping My goodLife
- Part 1a: Budgeting My goodLife's Planned Expenses
- Part 1b: Budgeting My goodLife's Unplanned Expenses
- Part 2: Budgeting My goodLife's Savings & Investments
- Part 3: Budgeting My goodLife's Debt Payoff
- Part 4: Budgeting My goodLife's Little Luxuries
- Part 5: Budgeting My Income for Income Allocation

Step 4 | Generating My goodLife Income

Step 5 | Establishing goodPractices for a goodLife

ex. 05.1

THOUGHTS & NOTES

ex. 05.1

Conclusion

The most fundamental human concern is survival. I believe that the second is freedom. Our survival and freedom are required to live a goodLife. We can survive without a lot of money, but we cannot thrive in all six life categories without a certain amount of it.

I believe that the attainment of freedom requires us to develop a healthy relationship with money. Any healthy relationship requires time, attention, respect and love—and that includes our relationship with money. We do this by vowing to respect money's laws and by giving it time and attention each month through the act of budgeting. We must learn to love money. I don't mean that you need to love money above and beyond everything and everyone else, but that you need to appreciate its capacity to support the cost of living a goodLife.

My relationship with money affords me the following:

My goodFaith

I hold a deep faith and feel connected to a universe far bigger than I am. I think it's this faith that gives me my resiliency. I believe I am on this earth for a reason and that my human virtue is to be the best Krisstina I can be. My commitment to always be becoming means that the Krisstina I am tomorrow will be a better version of the Krisstina I am today. My virtue is my ability to recognize and accept my lack of perfection as I continue on my journey of self-actualization and universal realization.

My goodFamily

I hold a deep, close, and connected relationship with my family. My marriage to Garry is beautiful. He is my partner in life. We know, because we've proven it, that even though life can give us ups and downs, we are in this together. I know he loves me for who I am, and who I'm not, and I love him in the same way.

The relationship I have with my two children touches my heart daily. It brings me such joy to see them grow into amazing, self-confident, and loving young adults about to embark on their own journey of self-actualization. As they commence their adulthoods, I offer them five fundamental pieces of advice:

- Forge your own path
- Never be afraid to fail
- Love with all your heart
- Make a difference
- Live a life of becoming the best Kael and Macy you can be

I am also lucky in that I am close with my parents. We had rough beginnings, but we've grown together. Today, my dad is the most loving, supportive, and giving man I know. My step-mom loves me like her own daughter. After being emotionally distant from my mother my entire life, we are closer now than ever and are both working to narrow the distance.

I have also recently begun to mend my troubled relationship with my brother. Our young abandonment flung us in different directions, literally and metaphorically. We were split up and grew up in different locations, breaking the bond we had when younger. I then followed the path of numbing my pain through perfectionism and accomplishment, while his numbing was carried out with drugs and alcohol. We appeared to be two completely different people, but we were (and are) actually much the same. I have learned to love and appreciate my brother for exactly who he is and am working to mend the bond that once existed.

My goodFinances

My income and net worth rank in the top 1% of Americans—quite a distance from where I began. If illustrated on a graph, you would see that the growth of my money has really been a roller coaster ride, with multiple ups and downs as it veered from one corner to the next.

I say this to point out that my income and worth have not always been in this bracket. More than once in my working adulthood I've had to drastically cut expenses and pare down my lifestyle. Yet, because Garry and I continued to work our plan while remaining committed to our saving and investing—even when times were slim—we were able to stay on track. Today we're in the best financial position of our lives thus far.

My goodFitness and goodHealth

I (now) hold love and respect for myself. I honor myself through self-care that consists of a disciplined approach to exercise, healthy food, meditation, therapy, massage, rest, recovery, and love.

The best thing I've done for myself is to forgive myself. Without realizing it, I carried the shame I acquired as a child long into adulthood. This subconscious shame manifested into my need to be perfect, meaning that good was never good enough. Living a life of perfection is not only impossible, but trying to do so is seriously unhealthy and promises unwanted future consequences. I've learned that it's possible to be ambitious, passionate, happy, and imperfect all at the same time.

The second best thing I've done recently for my self-care was one of the most dificult things I've ever done. I ended some unhealthy long-term relationships. This included a close friendship and several business relationships. The pain from cutting these close ties has only recently dissipated, but my quality of life and overall happiness jumped immediately after distancing myself from the effects of unhealthy relationships.

My goodFun

From my scary bout with illness, I gained a new appreciation for the word "fun." A couple of weeks after getting back from treatment, Wendy, one of my team members, said, "I love this new Krisstina!" I don't exactly know what she meant, but I attributed it to my new-found ability to laugh, play, and have fun. I've learned that I can be enormously successful without having to take myself too seriously. I now have a life outside of work and know how to play just for the fun of it. Who knew?

As a result of your own work, you have five new "assets" that you can use to make and keep more money. The tools, if used as suggested, can change your life just as they have changed mine. They will ensure that you live a goodLife today and in the future. Those tools are:

1. goodLife and dreamLife goals
2. goodLife Spending Map
3. goodLife Money Map
4. goodLife Income Allocation Map
5. goodLife Number

As Jim Rohn once wrote, "The philosophy of the rich versus the poor is this: the rich invest their money and spend what is left; the poor spend their money and invest what is left."

I'll add to that by saying this: most people overestimate what they can do financially in a year, but underestimate what they can do in a decade. You build wealth in decades, not days. My personal wealth-building methodology has built upon this and other money philosophies, as well as my own learned skills and applied practices. The result is my five-step Money Mapping System, which I use myself as a means to survive, to become financially free, and ultimately live a goodLife.

I have shared my personal stories here to illustrate that I've been able to create a goodLife despite my troubled upbringing and multitude of failures. If I've been able to reach the top 1% simply as a result of following a sound financial philosophy and committed financial practice, so can you.

Remember, wealth-building isn't a one-and-done experience. It takes persistent effort, constant reevaluation, and firm resilience.

You have to own it! I hope this book has inspired you to start your journey, and I've intended it to be a tool you can revisit often.

I also want to continue to be involved in your experience. Please feel free to interact with me and my team on social media or share your thoughts about money at wealthy-wellthy.com. I've created that website to be a great resource for you in designing, producing and living a goodLife in all six F categories.

If any of what I've shared with you thus far has positively impacted you, I am gratified. Using one of my teenage daughter's favorite phrases, "I'm not gonna lie." It's the truth: writing this book has been one of the most dificult challenges I've ever taken on. Its completion required a commitment (and associated pain) beyond what I had anticipated. But if I've offered you at least one Aha! moment, you've gifted me with enough reward to make it all worthwhile. I hope to hear from you soon.

Here's to living a goodLife.

Appendix

Step 1:
Reflecting on My goodLife | Chapter
My goodLife Reflection | Exercise

Step 2:
Setting My goodLife Goals | Chapter 2
Part 1: Visualizing My dreamLife | Exercise 2.1
Part 2: Setting My Annual goodLife Goals | Exercise 2.2

Step 3:
Money Mapping My goodLife | Chapter 3
Part 1: Budgeting My goodLife ARMe
    Step 1: Planning for My Planned Expenses | Exercise 3.1
    Step 2: Planning for the Unplanned | Exercise 3.2
Part 2: Budgeting My Savings & Investments | Exercise 3.3
Part 3: Budgeting My Debt Payoff | Exercise 3.4
Part 4: Budgeting My goodLife's Little Luxuries | Exercise 3.5
Part 5: Budgeting My Income for Allocation | Exercise 3.6

Step 4:
Generating My goodLife Income | Chapter 4
Setting My goodBusiness Goals | Exercise 4.1

Step 5:
Establishing goodPractices for a goodLife | Chapter 5
goodPractices for a goodLife | Exercise 5.1

Financial Best Practices Checklist

	GOAL	ACTUAL
My ARMe	$	$
Planned	$	$
Unplanned	$	$
My Savings	$	$
My Investments	$	$
My Luxuries	$	$

QUESTIONS TO ASK

- Can I reduce my ARMe expenses?

- How much debt have I paid off?

- How much am I saving?

- How much am I investing?

- What little luxuries can I go without until I'm on track with my saving and investing?

- How can I increase my income?

- What will I invest in? Real Estate, Index funds, PreTax Retirement plan?

- ○ Pay bills.

- ○ Sweep the monthly budgeted amounts for the different savings and investing commitments into the respective accounts.

- ○ Import actual expenses into budget.

- ○ Reconcile all accounts.

- ○ Assess the budget versus actual numbers, adjusting budget numbers if necessary.

- ○ Are there any action items? For example, can I make a call to a credit card company to try and get a lower interest rate?

QUARTERLY CHECKLIST

- ○ Review my Required ARMe expenses.

- ○ Reduce any Required ARMe expenses.
  For example, my cell phone is an ARMe expense, but can I lower the number of minutes?

- ○ Review the savings for Unplanned ARMe expenses.
  Do I need to replenish any withdrawn monies? If so, modify the budget accordingly.

- ○ Review the savings and investments accounts.
  How much do I have in savings? Is it growing? What is my net worth?

- ○ Assess investment account.
  Is it time to invest?

- ○ Review my debt payoff schedule.
  Am I reducing my debt?

Compounding Table

Years to Retirement	Current Investment Required to Earn $100,000 Annually at Retirement*	Minimum Annual Payment Required if $0 Invested Now*	Required if $0 Invested Now*
35	$169,086.36	$13,433.48	$1,082.64
34	$182,613.27	$14,592.85	$1,178.89
33	$197,222.33	$15,860.26	$1,284.33
32	$213,000.11	$17,247.25	$1,399.95
31	$230,040.12	$18,766.86	$1,526.86
30	$248,443.33	$20,433.87	$1,666.34
29	$268,318.80	$22,265.13	$1,819.85
28	$289,784.30	$24,279.87	$1,989.04
27	$312,967.05	$26,500.22	$2,175.82
26	$338,004.41	$28,951.68	$2,382.40
25	$365,044.76	$31,663.84	$2,611.33
24	$394,248.34	$34,671.21	$2,865.58
23	$425,788.21	$38,014.28	$3,148.66
22	$459,851.27	$41,740.90	$3,464.68
21	$496,639.37	$45,907.99	$3,818.58
20	$536,370.52	$50,583.82	$4,216.23
19	$579,280.16	$55,850.99	$4,664.77
18	$625,622.57	$61,810.41	$5,172.91
17	$675,672.38	$68,586.65	$5,751.41
16	$729,726.17	$76,335.35	$6,413.70
15	$788,104.26	$85,253.58	$7,176.79
14	$851,152.60	$95,594.57	$8,062.54
13	$919,244.81	$107,689.36	$9,099.52
12	$992,784.40	$121,979.21	$10,325.81
11	$1,072,207.15	$139,065.61	$11,793.33
10	$1,157,983.72	$159,790.48	$13,574.73
9	$1,250,622.42	$185,369.70	$15,774.95
8	$1,350,672.21	$217,626.76	$18,551.36
7	$1,458,725.99	$259,426.86	$22,151.19
6	$1,575,424.07	$315,544.88	$26,986.52
5	$1,701,457.99	$394,575.13	$33,798.99
4	$1,837,574.63	$513,705.57	$44,071.83
3	$1,984,580.60	$713,040.54	$61,265.81
2	$2,143,347.05	$1,112,891.74	$95,763.14
1	$2,314,814.81	$2,314,814.81	$199,474.58
0	$2,500,000.00	$2,500,000.00	$208,333.33

*This does not account for Inflatio

About the Author

Krisstina Wise is a real estate mogul, lifestyle entrepreneur and creator of several multi-million dollar businesses including GoodLife Realty, GoodLife Mortgage, and The Paperless Agent. She is also an international speaker and the author of the Amazon Best-Seller Falling for Money, a romance novel for your bank account. Named one of the 100 Most Influential Real Estate Leaders in the country, she has been featured in USA TODAY, as well as by Evernote and Apple for her creative leadership and technological innovations.

After nearly losing her life in 2013 and spending almost half a million dollars to get it back, she is ready to change the world again by inspiring others on how to build extraordinary wealth and find incredible health–the GoodLife–through cutting-edge, research based education, access to the world's top wealth strategists and doctors, private getaways for Power Couples and life-changing WealthyWellthy™ products.

33856567R00083

Made in the USA
Middletown, DE
29 July 2016